real life
CHRISTIANITY

Galatians 6:9

Alan Kelly

real life CHRISTIANITY

7 Basic Principles for Successful Christian Living

Alan Kelly

Tate Publishing & *Enterprises*

Real Life Christianity

Published by Tate Publishing & Enterprises, LLC
127 E. Trade Center Terrace | Mustang, Oklahoma 73064 USA
1.888.361.9473 | www.tatepublishing.com

Tate Publishing is committed to excellence in the publishing industry. The company reflects the philosophy established by the founders, based on Psalm 68:11,
"The Lord gave the word and great was the company of those who published it."

Cover design by Amber Gulilat
Interior design by Stefanie Rooney

Published in the United States of America

ISBN: 978-1-60799-710-8
1. Religion, Christian Life, Spiritual Growth
2. Religion, Christian Life, General
09.07.15

Dedication

This book is dedicated to the memory of my mother, Fern Kelly. She was the facilitator of the "drug" problem I had growing up. She "drug" me to church every time the doors were open.

Acknowledgments

Since we have been married for over thirty years, my first thank you has to go to my BFF, Janice. Without her strength and encouragement, there is no way I would be anywhere close to the man I am today. And my kids too: Jamie, Joey, Hillary, and my brand-new son-in-law, Ryan. What a great family I have!

Next on my list is Pastor Stan Morris; he has been our pastor twenty-two years now and has had a huge impact on who I am, who our family is, and how we all turned out. I count it a real privilege to have been part of the Family Worship Center family for all these years.

A very special thanks goes to his daughter, Sherri Leith. She took the time to read each chapter of my book as I finished it and then marked it up like an English teacher. I really needed that; it was a great help.

Then all the others that read my book and gave me their thoughts, observations, and helpful suggestions: Earl and Sharon Jernberg, Kathy Sullivan, Jim Simons, Jim Quigg, Janice, and Pastor Stan. You are the best!

And now I have a brand-new association in my life, Tate Publishing. I am thrilled that I have been invited to join that family too and am very excited to see how this all turns out.

Table of Contents

Foreword

Alan Kelly is a true man of God who for the last fifty years has been preparing himself for this book. Life is a preparation place for all of us. Coming out of the trenches of many years of developing a great gift, Alan has gifted the body of Christ with a book that is desperately needed in the church today. We see people come to Christ, and many times they do not know what they have received. The book *Real Life Christianity* is what people are looking for, and it is what new believers really need in their lives today. There have been so many hits against Christians and against Christianity that new believers don't really know what or whom they can trust.

You can trust this book. You can trust the author of this book. And you can trust the one this book tells us about. The author of *Real Life Christianity* has been tried and tested in the trenches of life. He has been married to his wife, Janice, for over thirty years. Alan has three children who are all serving God and developing the gifts in their own lives. This book will inspire and motivate new Christians to really dig in and find out what they have received when they receive Jesus as their Savior.

I am not overestimating the power of this great book when I confidently encourage you to embrace and implement its deep biblical truths into your life. It will change you, which will change your life.

The strategy our Lord employed and the one Alan Kelly advises in this book is to dig deeper into the love of God. You can go further and faster than you ever thought possible. Go with God!

—Dr. Stan M. Morris
Senior Pastor
Family Worship Center

Introduction

> These people honor me with their lips, but their hearts are far from me. Their worship is a farce, for they teach man-made ideas as commands from God.
>
> Mark 7:6–7 (NLT)

God is really not much into religion! I know that is kind of surprising to some, but let me put it this way: God is not impressed by our religious traditions. Our religions are mostly man-made attempts to try to get through to God. We get more wrapped up in rituals and traditions than serving God and living in obedience to him. All of the religious stuff we do has no impact on God if it is not accompanied by obedience to his Word. Most of us know very little about the Bible, so we think that religion is about a bunch of dos and don'ts that are hard to live up to. As far as we can tell, God just doesn't want us to have any fun.

Church and Christianity should be interesting, enjoyable, and should apply to our everyday, real lives. Most people do not usually associate church with fun; that's because religion has made it boring and irrelevant. It shouldn't be like that. I once heard a preacher say, "People don't need to hear more about theology and doctrine; they need to know how to get up Monday morning, get their pants on, and get to work on time." That is exactly right. If church is not about how to make our marriages work, how to raise our kids, how to be a good employee or good employer, then it is a waste of time. You might as well stay home because God is not going to respond to your religious sacrifice of attending church anyway.

What God is actually into is people. He is much more interested in you than he is in religion! He wants to have a daily relationship with you. Not a religion. He wants you to spend your days with him: eating breakfast together, paying your bills together, running errands together, taking care of your kids together, cleaning your house together, going to work together, and just enjoying life together. It is what you were designed for, and it is why you were created.

We can have a relationship with God because he came after us and provided a way for us to be brought back into friendship with him. There is nothing we can do to earn it. It comes because of what Jesus did for us. I believe that God actually hates religion when it makes people think that if they perform some religious ritual they will show God how much they love him and then he will love them back. God loves you no matter who you are, what you have done, or what you are doing. He loves you no matter where you are from and no matter what your race or religion is. He loves you no matter what your political beliefs are and no matter what your gender or sexual preference might be. He just loves you. And he wants to be part of your life.

Read the gospel accounts of Jesus while he was on earth. He made this statement: "Anyone who has seen me has seen the Father, because the Father and I are one" (John 14:9, NLT). So if you look to see what Jesus was like, you will find out what God is like. Here is what you need to know about Jesus: he loves people, he cares about people, he is interested in people, and he identifies with people. While he was on earth, he loved just hanging out with people. He loved going out to eat with them and he loved just sitting around visiting with them. He loved walking and talking with them and telling them stories. He loved teaching them, healing them, and praying for them.

Jesus has this to say about religion and religious leaders:

> What sorrow awaits you teachers of religious law and you Pharisees. Hypocrites! For you shut the door of the Kingdom of Heaven in people's faces. You won't go in yourselves, and you don't let others enter either ... You are so careful to clean the outside of the cup and the dish, but inside you are filthy—full of greed and self-indulgence! For you are like whitewashed tombs—beautiful on the outside but filled on the inside with dead people's bones and all sorts of impurity. Outwardly you look like righteous people, but inwardly your hearts are filled with hypocrisy and lawlessness.
>
> Matthew 23:13, 25, 27–28 (NLT)

Jesus struggled with religion, and religion struggled with him. It wasn't so much the Jewish religion that Jesus struggled with, as some would try to tell you; it was their religious attitudes.

There are a lot of ideas in this country about religion and Christianity. Many of them are very distorted, and a lot of that distortion comes from the Christians themselves. I have been teaching a class for new believers at our church for several years, and most of my students are quite surprised at what Christianity is really all about and what the Bible says about how we are to live our everyday lives. When people begin to understand what God wants for them and what a great life he has in store for them, they get excited. Though most doubt it could really happen to them, they do enjoy thinking about the possibilities.

I want to let everyone know something right up front. I am not a theologian, and I am not a senior pastor. I didn't even graduate from Bible college. Not that any of those are bad things, as a matter of fact, any of those are great goals to have and great accomplishments if you've already achieved one or more of them.

Actually, I am a shipyard worker. I am an employee at Puget Sound Naval Shipyard. I have been blessed, though, to have been involved in Christianity for my entire life. As a matter of fact, I was born on a Thursday, made it to church that very first Sunday, and I have been part of it ever since. In the summer when I was seven years old, I gave my heart to Jesus at Daily Vacation Bible School.

My wife, Janice, and I both grew up in Bremerton, Washington, and we married in 1978. Janice makes me think of the line from the movie *As Good As It Gets* when Jack Nicholson says, "You make me want to be a better man." She has brought a stability to my life that

I could never have achieved on my own. She began many years ago to speak good things into my life. She told me that I was a good man, that I was a good husband, and that I was a good father, even before I comprehended what any of that really meant. We have reached a point now where we are really enjoying life. We are learning and growing and being challenged every day, but at the same time life is very peaceful and enjoyable. I know we would have never reached this stage in our lives if very early in our marriage, Janice hadn't set a standard of discipline, responsibility, and excellence in whatever we put our hands to.

We have also been blessed with three unbelievable children. Our first, Hillary, was born in Germany in 1981 when I was serving in the US Army. We didn't realize it at the time, but her name is taken from the Greek word *hilaros,* which is where we get our English word *hilarious.* It means happy and cheerful, and it fits her to a tee. She is beautiful and smart, and you will very rarely find her without a smile on her face. She has such high standards that even her mom and I fall short from time to time. And she is not afraid to call us "slackers" if she catches us letting up or being lazy.

Hillary has two little brothers, Joey and Jamie. They were both born at Tacoma General Hospital, Joey in 1985, and Jamie in 1987. You couldn't find two more opposite personalities if you planned it that way. Joey is quiet and pretty shy, although he does like to clown around and get attention from being funny and silly. He took piano lessons when he was young and then learned to play the guitar when he was a teenager. He has become a very accomplished musician and plays lead guitar on our church worship team. I love to watch him play and am amazed at the remarkable sounds he can make come out of his "Fatstrat" (a type of Fender electric guitar).

Jamie is our youngest. He has the kind of personality that everyone loves to be around. He is friendly, happy, and he loves to be the center of attention. He is a musician too. He is a most excellent drummer and has learned to play the guitar and loves to sing too. When he was in high school, he was the worship leader in our church youth group. He is a hard worker and has big ideas and big plans for his life.

I'm sure that God has some amazing plans for each of our kids, and I love watching them develop and discover new things. Just like all of us, they make foolish choices from time to time and have to deal with the consequences of that, but hopefully they are learning from their experiences and growing, changing, developing, and discovering the destiny that God has created them for.

We all live in Port Orchard, Washington, and attend Family Worship Center. We started there at the church's very first service on the last Sunday of August in 1986. Janice and I have worked in just about every department in the church over the years: music, youth, Sunday school, children's ministries, men's ministries, women's ministries, ushering, and door greeting. In 1997 we started our own ministry through the church called Forever Together Marriage Ministries. That is what we do now and we love it. We teach marriage classes, organize and speak at retreats, have mentoring classes in our home, and occasionally do some counseling. I have also been on the Elder Board since the church started and would be considered what some churches might call a lay pastor. Janice and I also have a weekly small group meet in our home that our church calls a Life Group.

In spite of the advantage I have had of being around the things of God for my entire life and the great life God has given me now, I still manage to make enough silly or selfish decisions to cause trouble for all of us. I think sometimes that if it weren't for me and the kids, Janice would have a pretty simple and carefree life, but she's always got us around to keep things interesting.

My point in all of this is that I have been around Christianity for a long time and I have picked up a few things along the way. Most of what I've written in this book I've learned through years and years of listening to great teachers and preachers and reading their books. In the Bible God promises that he will add to our knowledge of his Word and his ways by the teaching and studying we do over the course of our lifetime. Not everybody has had the same advantages I've had. Most people are not very familiar with the Bible and the ways of God. That is why I wrote this book, to tell you about the basic principles of the Christian faith and to get you started on your process of learning all about God and what he has done for you. I want to let you know that it is actually all pretty straightforward and not at all as complicated as you might have thought.

The first three chapters of this book lay the foundation of our Christian beliefs. We'll start with the Bible, what it is, where it comes from, and why we believe it. Then we'll learn about God, who he is, and what he is really like. After that we'll find out about man, why we were created, and what an amazing creation we truly are. But then, in chapter four, the tension begins. What happened to God's special creation, and what separated us from the relationship with him we were designed for? What did God do then? What happened when he stepped in to restore that relationship and bring us back to himself? After that we'll learn about the great gift he gave us to maintain that special connection we have with him. Finally, we will find out how to take all of these teachings and truly apply them to our lives. We'll learn how to move past having a religious experience to experiencing a daily relationship with God.

When I sat down to write this book, it was with the brand-new Christian in mind. I want to give you a basic understanding of Christian theology and doctrine. But my real goal is to help you understand how our Christian faith applies to your everyday real life.

What I discovered however, is that this is actually for every Christian, no matter how long you have been saved. I even learned a few things myself as I was writing it. I think one of the shortcomings of our churches today is a lack of Bible knowledge in many Christians. Here is a basic theology course in easy-to-understand terms that can change your life if you learn to apply the principles. Our Christian doctrines and our theology are pretty useless if we don't know how to apply them to our lives.

If you are not a Christian, then I'm sure you're thinking, *This all sounds good if you are interested in that sort of thing, but I'm just not the religious type.* That's a good thing, because God is not the religious type either and he is not really interested in adding any more religious types to his team. He already has plenty.

I encourage all of you to read this book with an open mind. If you have doubts about God and Christianity, then I would like you to say this prayer as you begin to read: "God, if any of the information in this book is true, and it's not just a bunch of nonsense, then I pray that you reveal yourself to me as I read through these pages."

If you are new to Christianity or if you have been saved for a long time, ask God to give you an understanding of these basic beliefs and how to apply them to your life so you can grow and change. Then trust God to establish his promises in you. He is going to do some great things in your life.

Sincerely,

Alan Kelly
www.forevertogetheronline.com

The Word of God

> All Scripture is inspired by God and is useful to teach us what is true and to make us realize what is wrong in our lives. It corrects us when we are wrong and teaches us to do what is right. God uses it to prepare and equip his people to do every good work.
>
> 2 Timothy 3:16–17 (NLT)

Principle 1 - As Christians we believe that the Bible is the inspired Word of God. We base our entire lives and everything we believe on its teachings.

This is a very important concept for people to understand. Without the guiding principles of the Bible, there is no basis for our beliefs or our way of life. On top of that it has to be completely true, or none of it is true. How do we know that the Bible really is the book we say it is? If you stay with me, I am going to explain a few things to you about the Bible. Things that you may have never heard before or might not have understood. I believe I can explain the Bible in such a way that you will come to the realization that you can believe the Bible is real, it is true, and you can trust it completely. Here are four pieces of evidence that show the Bible is true and that it is the very words of God himself.

The Amazing History of the Bible

What is this book? Where did it come from? Why should we believe a collection of ancient writings? And what makes it any different than any of the other ancient books in the world?

I once had a friend ask the question "Why should I believe a book that some guy wrote thousands of years ago?"

And when asked, "Who do you think wrote it?" he replied, "I don't know, King James, I guess."

Now to most people that seems perfectly logical. The few of us, however, that really know a little about the Bible realize that his thoughts about it are kind of foolish. So when we hear comments like that, we chuckle to ourselves and wink knowingly, while the rest of society asks, "What's so funny?"

The sad part is that the vast majority of people know very little about the Bible and see no reason why they should. Of course people in other parts of the world, where they practice completely different religions, don't know anything about the Bible. Why would they? I'm talking about people here in the Western world, where much of our culture and our laws have their roots in Christianity and where a large portion of our population considers themselves religious and even attends church from time to time.

As a culture, our overall knowledge of the Bible is very limited. What is even sadder is that those of us who do have some knowledge of the Bible don't share it with everyone we know. We realize the huge impact it had on our lives when we learned to live in obedience to it, yet we keep it to ourselves.

So let's take a look at this amazing book. The first thing you need to know is that it is not one book; it is a collection of many books, sixty-six to be exact. They were written by over forty different authors over a period of about 1500 years, from approximately 1400 b.c. to 100 a.d. These authors came from many different backgrounds including kings, shepherds, statesmen, prophets, priests, fishermen, and even a tent maker. There is a common theme though that runs throughout the Bible in each of its books—God sending his Son, Jesus Christ, into the world to rescue us from a life of failure and hopelessness.

Many religions are based on a book written by the originator of the religion, like the writings of Confucius or Buddha or the Koran written by the prophet Muhammad. Christianity is based on the life and teachings of Jesus Christ, but he did not write any of the Bible.

The Bible is divided into two sections. The first is called the Old Testament, and it contains thirty-nine of the books. It was written in the ancient Hebrew language. In the first few chapters of the very first book, it tells about the creation of the world, the first people, and the story of Noah's flood. But it quickly moves on to beginnings of the nation of Israel, and then the rest of the Old Testament tells us the history of that great nation.

The second section is called the New Testament, and it contains the remaining twenty-seven books of the Bible. All of it was written in the first century AD. Some of it was written in Aramaic, which was the language in Israel at that time, but most of it was written in Greek, which was the language of most of the people who lived in the eastern part of the Roman Empire, where Israel was located. The first four books tell about the life and the teachings of Jesus and were written by some of his followers. The next book tells the story of his followers as they formed what is called the "early church." The rest of the books contain the teachings of his followers, written in the form of letters that were sent to other believers in churches around that area.

From the very beginning, Jewish and then Christian scholars had translated and copied the ancient Scripture texts. Men known as scribes would sit and copy Scriptures by hand, over and over until there were thousands of copies of both the Old and New Testaments. Remember, the printing press would not be invented until hundreds of years later.

Because the New Testament was largely written in Greek and scholars had also translated the Old Testament into Greek, the gospel message spread quickly around the Roman Empire of the first century AD. However, by the second century, Christians began to realize that if they were to take the gospel message any further in the world, the Bible would need to be translated into more languages. They set to work and soon translations in Latin, Coptic, Gothic, Armenian, Ethiopic, Georgian, Syriac, and many other languages of the time began to appear.

Any religion, though, that did not support the worship of the emperor was illegal in the Roman Empire. Because of that, Christians, Jews, and anyone else that would not endorse the philosophy of emperor worship were imprisoned, tortured, and killed. To avoid persecution, the Christian church stayed underground. Even though they had to live in hiding, the church still flourished and spread around the known world. This difficult life for Christians continued without much change for about three hundred years. Then something happened that would change Christianity forever.

Constantine was named emperor of the western part of the Roman Empire in AD 306. A man named Maxentius was emperor of the eastern part. Constantine would have been happy to leave it like that, but Maxentius was not. In 312 he declared war on Constantine with the intention of claiming the entire Roman Empire for himself. On the day before Constantine's army went to battle with Maxentius, his mother went to him and told him to pray to the God of the Christians. Apparently she had had some exposure to Christianity, so he followed her advice. He was willing to try anything because he knew he was severely outmanned by the Maxentius's forces. That night he had a vision. A large cross appeared in the sky over the fighting that would take place the next day. There were words written across it that read, *"By this sign you will conquer."* The next day he won the battle easily and became the sole emperor of the Roman Empire.

His mother became a devout Christian. At her prompting, Constantine made it illegal to persecute Christians, or any other religion for that matter, in the Roman Empire. Later he named Christianity the official religion of the Roman Empire, and it became known as the Roman Catholic (universal) Church. This, of course, didn't make anyone in the empire a Christian, but it did give the new universal church the freedom to grow and spread throughout the world without fear and without persecution.

Over time the church became more structured and organized and developed a hierarchy of church leadership. It is unclear through historical accounts of the church exactly how and when, but they chose to put one man in charge of the entire church, and he became known as the Pope (*Papa* in Latin and *Pappas* in Greek. Both mean father).

Most of the western part of the Roman Empire now spoke Latin, and because of that, there were several Latin translations of both the Old and New Testaments available for use. There were many variations in the different translations, and the official church considered this to be confusing and divisive. In 382, in an effort to bring some unity to the churches, Pope Damascus I commissioned a monk named Jerome to come up with one official Latin translation of the Bible. It was the first Latin translation to use the ancient Hebrew manuscripts of the Old Testament rather than the newer Greek translations. It was an excellent translation of the Bible, and it became known as the Vulgate Version.

For awhile things were going very well for the Christians, but eventually true Christianity—the personal relationship with God through Jesus Christ—began to disappear. The universal church was now becoming a more formal religion with its center of operations in Rome. Over the years the church began to discourage translations of the Bible into other languages, and it made Jerome's translation the only version that could be used in religious services. Those who tried to convey the gospel in any other language but Latin were discouraged, persecuted, and even put to death. The gospel that once spoke to the common man in his own language became unknown and foreign to those unable to speak Latin. When access to the teachings of God can only come through the religious leaders, the people are left to believe whatever the teachers and leaders tell them to believe, whether it is true or not.

It soon became illegal even to try to approach God without going through the church. The church was now developing a thirst for power and control. Using fear and intimidation and often preying on the faith and the fears of the people, it was able to gain control over nations and governments. It was able to control the money, the land, and all of the people completely. The unintended result of the church's tightfisted control over all of society was a time of extreme poverty and superstition. As a matter of fact, you probably learned in school that this dark period of time is known as the Dark Ages. This was a time when culture and society seemed to take a giant step backwards from the great civilizations of the Romans, the Greeks, the Babylonians, and the Egyptians. All because the light, the Word of God, was taken out of the hands of the people.

Throughout this period in history are stories of men and women who were able to get their hands on all or just portions of the Bible. When they read for themselves and understood the Scriptures, they came to realize that true Christianity is all about a personal relationship with God and not what religion you belong to. Whenever these people went against or did not listen to and obey the rules and regulations handed down by the "official" church, they were branded as heretics and arrested. If they would not deny their faith and swear their allegiance to the Holy Catholic Church, they were imprisoned and often executed.

Eventually some men came along who were able to stand up to the Catholic Church. These men were scholars, so they had access to the Scriptures that most of the common people did not. Because of their education, they were able to read and study the Bible and came to realize that things were not right in the Christian world.

One of the earliest was John Wycliffe. Born in Yorkshire, England, in 1324, he entered Oxford University at only thirteen years of age. He was a brilliant scholar, and his studies covered a wide range of fields including chemical analysis, the physiological genesis of sleep, geometrical and mathematical rules, and the workings of the human eye. He is credited with the invention of bifocals.

In his early adulthood he came under the influence of a man named Thomas Bradwardine. Mr. Bradwardine understood what many others of his time seemed to be unaware of, that the Bible was the revealed Word of God and that each individual had access to God and his forgiveness. When he explained all of this to his new student, John Wycliffe was captivated. He then began to act on his newfound faith and speak out to the people of England about the truths in God's Word. His influence in the nation soon began to grow, and because he was not only knowledgeable but a gifted speaker as well, he was soon in demand all over England. He was widely respected at Oxford and influential among several members of parliament. His popularity inevitably led to conflict with the Catholic Church, and the rest of his life was one of turmoil and trouble. The pope and his supporters were furious with him and issued orders to have him imprisoned and punished for coming against the teachings of the church. However, he had developed a strong ally in the king of England, and as long as King Edward III was alive, Wycliffe was protected from the church leaders. But when the king passed away in 1377, his favor came to an end. He was expelled from Oxford and retired to a place called Lutterworth. There he completed his life's dream of translating the Bible from Latin into

English. Then, during a church service in 1384, he suffered a stroke and two days later passed away. He was still very popular among the people of England, and his influence was still felt long after his passing. Forty years after his death, a church council that was angry about his sway over the people gave the order to have his bones dug up and publicly burned. His ashes were then thrown into the Swift River. Their foolish act backfired, though, and his popularity grew to even greater heights. His influence in England was felt for over two hundred years.

Martin Luther was a Roman Catholic priest from Germany. He lived from 1483 to 1546. In his early years of ministry, he studied and preached messages from the books of Psalms, Hebrews, Romans, and Galatians. In his studies he began to realize that salvation is a gift of God's grace through Christ and received by faith alone. He wrote an article that stated, "Jesus Christ, our God and Lord, died for our sins and was raised again for our justification ... therefore, it is clear and certain that this faith alone justifies us." In 1517 he wrote a letter called the *Ninety-five Theses* and sent it to Albert, archbishop of Mainz and Magdeburg, in part to protest the ritual of paying for "indulgences." People would pay vendors working for the church to buy "relics" in order to get their loved ones who had passed away from purgatory into heaven. These relics were objects that were alleged to hold some spiritual significance because they were supposedly found in the Holy Land and dated from Bible times. He heard a priest say, "As soon as the coin in the coffer rings, the soul from purgatory springs." His letter was also posted on the door to his church. It was taken and copied and spread throughout Germany. His message of faith plus his *Ninety-five Theses* resulted in a flood of opposition from the church leaders, and it caused a firestorm in his own life.

His life was now at risk, and in 1521 he was taken into protective custody by a powerful landowner named Frederick the Wise. He was hidden in the Wartburg Castle at Eisenach, where he stayed for about a year. While he was there, he translated the New Testament from Greek to German. It was published in 1522. After he was able to leave the castle, he worked with a group of scholars to translate the entire Bible into German. It was published in 1534.

His followers became known as Lutherans, and this was the beginning of the Lutheran denomination. His followers and others who were springing up around the world were also called Protestants because they were protesting against the Catholic Church.

William Tyndale was born in North Nibley, England, in 1494. He was descended from an ancient Northumbrian family and attended school at Oxford, just as John Wycliffe had done about one hundred and fifty years earlier, but he actually graduated from Cambridge. He was a student of language and spoke at least five languages fluently. There is no record of him being ordained into ministry, but he was a devoted student of the Scriptures and followed the Reformation very closely. He preached openly of his beliefs and soon found himself at odds with the Catholic Church.

With his life under threat, he left England in 1523 and moved to Germany. Martin Luther's translation of the New Testament had a big impression on Tyndale. He had already been convinced that there needed to be an English version that was directly translated from the original languages instead of from the Latin version as Wycliffe had done. So he set to work and with Wycliffe's translation of the New Testament and Luther's German translation to aid his understanding of the ancient languages, Tyndale was able to translate the New Testament into English.

However, by this time something had happened that began to change everything. A German man named Johann Gutenberg had invented the printing press. Martin Luther's Bible was printed and distributed throughout Germany, and William Tyndale was able to have six thousand copies of his English New Testament smuggled back into England. He was now considered an enemy of the church and had to live in hiding, but he still began to study ancient Hebrew so he could translate the entire Bible into English. He was able to complete large portions of the Old Testament, and early transcripts of Luther's German translation helped him here also. However, in 1535, before he was able to complete his work, he was discovered and thrown into prison in Brussels. He was kept in prison for five hundred days, then strangled, and his body tied to a stake and burned. Two of his colleagues, John Rogers and Myles Coverdale, completed his work and had the entire Bible published in English in 1537. John Rogers used the pseudonym "Thomas

Matthew," and the work was distributed throughout England as the Matthew's Bible. This saved the English the embarrassment of using a Bible translated by William Tyndale.

Tyndale is considered by many to be the primary architect of the modern English Language. He had to invent many of the words and phrases he used in translating the Bible from the ancient languages into English. Large numbers of them have become so common that they have become part of our modern culture. Words like: Jehovah, Passover, atonement, and scapegoat. And the phrases: "Let there be light," "Eat, drink, and be merry," "The powers that be," "A prophet has no honor in his own country," "Ye of little faith," "Fight the good fight," "Am I my brother's keeper?", "The spirit is willing," "The salt of the earth," "A law unto themselves," "A man after his own heart," and "Signs of the times." William Tyndale.com[1] states: "It is surprising that the name of William Tyndale is not more familiar, for there is no man who did more to enrich the English language. Tyndale is the man who taught England how to read and showed Shakespeare how to write. No English writer—not even Shakespeare—has reached so many."

An amazing thing happened as these men and others were able to get the Word of God back into the hands of the people. It was no coincidence that the Renaissance or "Age of Enlightenment" began to take place at that exact time, because the light of God's Word was able to shine into the hearts of men and women everywhere.

These were very interesting and tumultuous times in the country of England. It was also a very interesting time for the Christians. But because of the turmoil, it was also a very difficult time for them. At that time the kings and queens of England were in complete control of their government. Things are quite different in today's world where royalty is really nothing more than a figurehead position that has very little to do with actually running the country. It seems that now they don't have much purpose other than to provide entertainment for the world and stories for the gossip magazines.

Henry VIII became King of England in 1509 when the country was firmly under the control of the Catholics. His first wife was Catherine of Aragon, and in 1516 they had a daughter named Mary. In 1527 he tried to have his marriage with Catherine annulled. He claimed it was because of a short marriage that Catherine had in her youth, but it was actually because she was getting older and still had not given Henry a son. The pope refused to allow his annulment. Henry had been in conflict with the pope and the Catholic Church for some time, and this was the last straw. He decided that the Church of England would no longer be Catholic and run by the pope; it would instead be Protestant with him in charge. He dissolved the monasteries and abbeys throughout England and appointed his friend Thomas Cranmer as the archbishop of Canterbury. Cranmer gave the king his annulment. Henry wasn't necessarily interested in the Protestant movement of the men like William Tyndale, John Rogers, and Myles Coverdale, but he didn't want the Catholics running England either. Even to this day, the king or queen of England is considered to be the head, at least symbolically, of the Church of England.

After his marriage to Catherine was annulled, Henry married a woman named Anne Boleyn and together they had a daughter named Elizabeth. She was their only child; and Henry wanted a son, so he had Anne Boleyn executed on a trumped-up charge of adultery, and he married a woman named Jane Seymour. She finally gave Henry his son when Edward was born in 1537. However, only ten short years later, Henry passed away, and the boy became King of England. There were some powerful men in the Church of England who had a strong influence over the boy king, and the country became very Protestant. However, the young man died of tuberculosis at only sixteen years of age.

When he died, the Protestants tried to name Lady Jane Grey as the queen, but by this time Henry's daughter Mary had developed some pretty strong allies of her own. Lady Jane had only been on the throne for nine days when Mary was able to seize control and take it away from her.

Queen Mary I and her friends were very strong Catholics, and they were determined to turn England back to Catholicism. To make a statement, she had both John Rogers, the man who had helped finish William Tyndale's Bible, and Thomas Cranmer, the man her father had appointed archbishop of Canterbury, executed. She then married King Philip II of Spain in the hopes that together they could create a kingdom and a son to be heir to their throne.

She began to have Protestants all over England arrested and imprisoned. She had nearly three hundred of them executed by burning them at the stake. That earned her the nickname "Bloody Mary." The Christians fled the country by the thousands, and many of them ended up in Switzerland. However, her reign was a short one because she died of an ovarian cyst after only five years on the throne, and her sister, Elizabeth, became the queen.

Elizabeth I took the throne in 1558 and quickly returned the nation to Protestantism. During the reign of Mary, while in exile in Switzerland, the Christians, led by a man named John Calvin, produced another English translation of the Bible. It was called the Geneva Bible. It largely contained the words of William Tyndale, but it was the first Bible to have the chapter and verse designations that we still see today. It also had marginal notes and commentaries to help the readers understand the Scriptures. Some of the comments were very political and definitely anti-Catholic. This Bible made its debut in 1560, and it was dedicated to Queen Elizabeth I of England. It was also the first Bible to be mass produced and very accessible to anyone who wanted it, and as a result it became extremely popular.

Because of the political comments in the Geneva Bible, it was never as popular with the church leaders as it was with the people. They put out a version of their own called the Bishop's Bible; but it never really caught on, and the Geneva Bible continued to grow in popularity.

Elizabeth had a successful forty-four-year reign as queen of England, and even though she fought wars against both France and Spain, it was a largely peaceful and prosperous time. It was the time of William Shakespeare and the explorers Sir Francis Drake and Sir Walter Raleigh. She was quite popular with the people of England and became known as Good Queen Bess. She never married, though, and was the last of the Tudor family to serve on the throne of England.

Toward the end of her life, Elizabeth became worried that after she died, England would return to the same tumultuous days it had been in before her reign. She appointed her second cousin King James VI of Scotland as king. He became King James I of England in 1603. His mother, Mary Queen of Scots, was a first cousin of Elizabeth's father, Henry VIII. James had been king in Scotland for twenty-nine years, and he ruled in England for twenty-two more. He was never truly accepted by the people of England and was not a very effective king. He married Princess Ann of Denmark, and together they had seven children.

He hated the Geneva Bible because of the political comments in it, so much so that he considered it a threat to his throne. When he was approached in 1604 by a group of scholars about the prospect of putting together a new translation of the Bible, he was thrilled. He told them, "*I profess I could never yet see a*

Bible well translated in English; but I think that, of all, the Geneva is the worst."

So the Bible scholars set to work, and in 1611 the "Authorized Version" of the Bible was introduced. It still contained much of the wording of William Tyndale, and it had the chapter and verse designations of the Geneva Bible, but it had no marginal notes or comments. The king was very excited about it, but the people of England greeted it with a collective yawn. They wanted nothing to do with a Bible put out by "that Scotsman."

The Geneva Bible continued to be the Bible of the people, and when the Pilgrims came to America in 1620, they brought the Geneva Bible. It was the primary version in America for over two hundred years because the Americans also weren't thrilled with the idea of using the Bible authorized by the king of England.

Eventually, however, the Authorized Version, or King James Version as it later became known, was the only Bible being published. Over time it came to be accepted, and its popularity grew until it finally became everyone's Bible. It has gone on to become the number-one most-sold book in the English language of all time.

Down through the centuries, there have been countless attempts to abolish the Bible and eliminate those who wrote it and those who have translated it. The Bible has been burned and buried and hidden away, but it will always continue to endure. In the Bible, it says, "The grass withers, the flower fades, but the word of our God stands forever" (Isaiah 40:8, NKJV). No one will ever succeed who tries to take it out of the hands of his people.

The countless unnamed monks and scribes who have sat by the hour, hidden in caves or tucked away in monasteries, have seen to it that we will always have God's Word to "provide a lamp unto our feet and a light unto our path" (Psalm 119:105, NKJV). It is estimated that there are over twenty-five thousand copies of the ancient manuscripts that were meticulously and painstakingly copied by these great men. By comparison there are only about five copies of *The Iliad,* the great epic that was written by the Greek writer Homer.

God also intended that his Word would be written in a language that his people could understand with ease. For instance the Greek language that was used in writing the New Testament is at the same level we use in the writing of our daily newspapers, while other ancient writings, like *The Iliad,* are in a language more comparable to a college textbook.

That is why it is important that we have access to other more modern translations of the Bible than only the King James Version we were just talking about. *Foxe's Book of Martyrs*[2] tells us that early in his life, William Tyndale went to his local church leaders to seek permission to translate the New Testament into English. When the priest denied his request, Tyndale responded angrily, "*If God spares my life, I will cause a boy that driveth the plough to know more of the Scripture than thou doest.*" He then made it his life's purpose to create a translation of the Bible that could be understood by the common people and the villagers of England. Now, 500 years later, we still need to be able to read and understand the Bible easily, but we don't speak or read that same language that Tyndale used when translating the Bible into English. God wants you and your children to be able to pick up the Bible, read it, comprehend it easily, and apply its teachings to your life.

Have you ever heard someone ask a question like, "Why should I believe a book that has been translated so many times?" Maybe you have asked that question yourself. The truth is that many people are confused about what a translation is and why there are so many of them.

A true translation of the Bible always goes back to the original texts. It will probably use others like the Latin translations or the Hebrew translated into Greek to help with the translation, but they will always translate from the original language to whatever language they are translating to, like German, Spanish, English, Russian, or whatever. So even though there are many translations, they are actually only translated once from the ancient language to the modern language.

There are many good modern English translations. As a matter of fact, because of the vast amount of archeological discoveries that have taken place in the last one hundred years, Bible scholars know more about the ancient languages now than they did five hundred years ago when they were first translating the Bible into other languages.

Here is a list of some of the most popular and reliable translations:

- The New American Standard Version (NASV)
- The New King James Version (NKJV)
- The New International Version (NIV)
- The New Living Translation (NLT)

There is another style of Bible called a paraphrase version. Instead of translating the Bible word for word, the author will attempt to convey the thoughts and ideas of the Bible into modern, easy-to-read language and modern ways of thinking and communicating. These can be enjoyable to read and can add clarity and understanding to the Scriptures but they would not be considered as reliable as a direct translation. Two of the more popular paraphrases are the Living Bible and the Message Bible.

My message to you is this: whichever one you choose, start now; read and study your Bible. Sometimes it helps in your understanding to study more than one of them. It is also good if you can get the one your pastor normally preaches out of. The one I have heard used most often is the New King James Version. Lately, I have really enjoyed reading the New Living Translation. It is the latest one, and I have even heard some preachers using it.

If you are looking at the store for a Bible, you might notice some titles like The Life Application Bible, The Spirit-Filled Life Bible, The Open Bible, or maybe The Thompson Chain Reference Bible. There are actually many others, and these titles are referring to editor comments and footnotes placed throughout the Bible to help you understand it as you are reading and studying. You will notice that you will have your choice of several translations, like the King James Version, the New King James Version, the New International Version, the New American Standard Version, or the New Living Translation in each of these formats.

The Bible Claims to be the Word of God

I know if you have doubts, then the previous points about the history of the Bible did not in itself convince you about the authenticity of the Bible. Here, though, is the most valid argument of all. The Bible itself claims to be the Word of God.

> All Scripture is inspired by God and is useful to teach us what is true and to make us realize what is wrong in our lives. It corrects us when we are wrong and teaches us to do what is right. God uses it to prepare and equip his people to do every good work.
>
> 2 Timothy 3:16 (NLT)

Another way to describe "inspired by God" is "God breathed." In other words, every verse in the Bible has come from the very breath of God. God inspired or breathed on men and caused them to write down the words of God. That verse explains that the Word of God has been given to us to teach us the difference between right and wrong and to prepare us to live such good lives that we have a positive impact on others.

> For the word of God is alive and powerful. It is sharper than the sharpest two-edged sword, cutting between soul and spirit, between joint and marrow. It exposes our innermost thoughts and desires.
>
> Hebrews 4:12 (NLT)

Here we learn the Bible is more than a book full of words; it is alive. When you read a book, you learn things, and it impacts your mind. When you read the Bible, you not only learn things with your mind; you are affected deep within your spirit.

There are over 2600 times in the Bible that it uses the phrase "and God said" or "the Lord said" or something similar. So the Bible is claiming to make direct quotes from God. The writers themselves often make the statement that they are writing the words of God.

When Jesus was on earth, he lived in obedience to the teachings of the Old Testament. Then he made this statement: "And the very words I have spoken to you are spirit and life" (John 6:63, NLT). He made the claim many times that he was God, and he gave his own words the same status as all of the other scriptures in the Bible.

Many of the books in the New Testament were written by the followers of Jesus. While he was still with them, Jesus made this promise to them: "But I will send you the Advocate—the Spirit of truth. He will come to you from the Father and will testify all about me" (John 15:26, NLT). Then he says, "When the Spirit of truth comes, he will guide you into all truth. He will not speak on his own but will tell you what he has heard. He will tell you about the future" (John 16:13, NLT).

So Jesus was telling his followers that after he left them he would send the Holy Spirit to them to remind them of everything he had done and said while he was on earth. Then he told them that the Holy Spirit would guide them into all truth. The books his disciples wrote were the truth they had been given by the inspiration of the Holy Spirit

The Influence the Bible has had on our World

The Bible has had a huge impact on the world we live in, especially in our Western society. Many of our ideas of government come from the Greek and Roman Empires. But our concept of rights and freedom and justice come from our own Judeo/Christian principles. In other words, they come from the Bible. Our societies are built around the assumptions of justice and fair play. We just know deep down inside that everybody ought to be treated right and that they deserve a decent chance in life.

> There is no longer Jew or Gentile, slave or free, male or female. For you are all one in Christ Jesus.
>
> Galatians 3:28 (NLT)

Isn't that a great concept? We are all the same, at least in God's eyes. We all have equal rights. It doesn't matter what our status in life is. It doesn't matter about our gender. Did you know it would have been impossible for there to have been a women's movement anywhere in the world or at any other time in world history except for our modern Western society? In most of the world and throughout most of history, women have been treated as second-class citizens and valued as nothing more than property. But because of the influence of Christianity and the values taught in the Bible, women are protected and valued in our culture. Now it hasn't always been perfect, and in some ways we still have a lot to learn; but for the most part, women are free to learn and grow and pursue whatever career or whatever interest they desire.

Many people have developed some very wrong concepts about the Bible and its teachings. The majority of those wrong ideas come from people's bad behavior and not what the Bible really teaches. Because the Bible says that wives should submit to their husbands, men have used that as justification to control and dominate women. The Bible does not give them that right, but through misinterpretation and selfish manipulation of the Word of God, men, even Christian men, have been able to get away with it.

What does the Bible really say?

> And give thanks for everything to God the Father in the name of our Lord Jesus Christ. And further, submit to one another out of reverence for Christ.
>
> Ephesians 5:20–21 (NLT)

This is actually the verse right before the one that says wives should submit to their husbands. It almost sounds like a partnership, doesn't it? Imagine that! Husbands and wives submitting to each other instead of living to meet their own selfish desires. Maybe God does know how to make a marriage work.

> For husbands, this means love your wives, just as Christ loved the church. He gave up his life for her.
>
> Ephesians 5:25 (NLT)

So here we see that a husband is supposed to love his wife. And he is supposed to put the same priority on her that Jesus puts toward his church (all Christians). A few years ago when the Promise Keepers movement was so big, we saw women's groups protesting outside their events because they thought that men were trying to hold women back somehow and keep them in the kitchen, barefoot and pregnant. Nothing could have been further from the truth. It was about men learning their roles as husbands and fathers and actually being taught to put their wives and children at the top of their priority lists, ahead of their jobs, golf, football, TV, cars, hunting, or whatever else men find to fill their time with.

I guess the point I am trying to make here is that just because people, even those who claim Christianity, assert that the Bible justifies their bad behavior, it doesn't make it true. The Bible teaches justice and fairness for everyone, and that is reflected in our laws and our culture.

For a civilization to be truly free, people have to live their lives under constraint. We have rights and freedom, but we also have responsibilities. Our rights cannot intrude in the rights and freedoms of others. A person who truly lives the ideals of Christianity will be part of the solution to society's ills rather than part of the problem.

But God has blessed our Western civilization. Even though we can look back through our history and find many inexcusable and unspeakably horrifying events that have taken place, as a society we have shown that we will not tolerate those kinds of evil for very long and that we will stand up and fight for the freedom and justice of the downtrodden. After the fall of the Roman Empire, and because of the influence of Christianity, Western civilization has grown to dominate the world. Regardless of all our unfortunate and destructive choices, in spite of our corrupt and greedy motivations, and even though we pay no attention to what God has done for us, he has blessed our many countries. Our people are the most successful and prosperous in the history of the world.

Not every single person is living the ideal life, but as an overall society we are doing well. And believe it or not, the opportunity is there for anyone, if they were to change and start making better choices in life to succeed and do well. There are probably some of you reading this who don't believe what I am saying right here. To you life is hard, and you see no way out of the deep hole you find your life in right now. I would challenge you to stay with me as we go through this book. Maybe I can show you where some of your difficult circumstances are coming from, and hopefully I will be able to give you some actual positive steps you can take that will change your life forever.

Because of our affluence, at least when compared with the way most of the rest of the world lives, God expects a lot from us.

> When someone has been given much, much will be required in return; and when someone has been entrusted with much, even more will be required.
>
> Luke 12:48 (NLT)

So, the more we have, the more that is required of us. We have been given an awful lot, and God expects us to reach out to others, to those around us when we see a need, and to those around the world who live desperate lives of sickness and poverty. The thing is, as long as you live a life of giving and helping, God will make sure you have the resources you need to help even more.

> You must each decide in your own heart how much you should give. And don't give reluctantly or in response to pressure. For God loves the person who gives cheerfully. And God will generously provide all you need. Then you will always have everything you need and plenty left over to share with others. As the Scriptures say, "They share freely and give generously to the poor. Their good deeds will be remembered forever."
>
> 2 Corinthians 9:7–9 (NLT)

But if you live in selfishness and greed, then even what resources you have will eventually dry up and go away.

> If you try to hang on to your life, you will lose it. But if you give up your life for my sake, you will save it.
>
> Matthew 16:25 (NLT)

This is Jesus talking. What do you think he means when he asks us to give up our life for him? Here are some more of the words of Jesus from the book of Matthew that I think spell that out pretty well:

> Then the King will say to those on the right, "Come, you who are blessed by my Father, inherit the Kingdom prepared for you from the creation of the world. For I was hungry, and you fed me. I was thirsty, and you gave me a drink. I was a stranger, and you invited me into your home. I was naked, and you gave me clothing. I was sick, and you cared for me. I was in prison, and you visited me."
>
> Then these righteous ones will reply, "Lord, when did we ever see you hungry and feed you? Or thirsty and give you something to drink? Or a stranger and show you hospitality? Or naked and give you clothing? When did we ever see you sick or in prison, and visit you?" And the King will say, "I tell you the truth, when you did it to one of the least of these my brothers and sisters, you were doing it to me!"
>
> Matthew 25:34–40 (NLT)

I believe that is why our Western societies have been so blessed. As a people we are very generous and willing to help others. We not only are willing to give financially, we are willing to give our time, and sometimes we are even willing to give our lives.

The Bible Has Changed Our Lives

Our lives are changed when we choose to live in obedience to God's Word. I know this point is subjective and rather hard to prove scientifically. That doesn't make it any less true, and it might be the most powerful proof of all.

Over the course of my lifetime in church, I have seen a lot of people come and go. Here is what I know: Those people who come to Jesus and learn to make good choices by being obedient to God's Word have seen things happen in their lives that they never dreamed possible. I have also seen people in the church who continue to lead lives of confusion and struggle. The usual reason is an inability or an unwillingness to change. If you were to ask them, they will probably tell you that Christianity and the teachings of God don't really work, at least for them. The reality, though, is that it is their unwillingness to apply the teachings of the Word of God that has stopped them.

There are many promises in the Bible about choosing to live under the blessing. This is one of my favorites. It comes from the book of Joshua in the Old Testament.

> This Book of the Law shall not depart from your mouth, but you shall meditate in it day and night,

> that you may observe to do according to all that is written in it. For then you will make your way prosperous, and then you will have good success.
>
> Joshua 1:8 (NKJV)

See that? We need to study and meditate on the Word of God. Why? So we learn more theological stuff about God? No! We study it so we can live in obedience to it. It is hard to obey rules we don't know anything about!

Why do we need to obey these rules? God didn't give us a bunch of rules and regulations just to make our lives boring and miserable. He laid out the guidelines and principles we need to live by in order to make our lives successful. As a matter of fact, God promised us in that verse that if we live in obedience to his word, we will be able make our way prosperous and we will have good success. What more do we need out of life than that? To be prosperous and successful. Successful in our marriages. Successful with our families. Successful on the job. Successful in life.

Here is another promise along that same line:

> If you are willing and obedient you shall eat the good of the land.
>
> Isaiah 1:19 (NKJV)

More proof that we need to know the rules. God promised that if we are willing to live in obedience to his Word we are going to have the best. But why does God want to bless us?

> And you shall remember the LORD your God, for it is He who gives you power to get wealth that He may establish His covenant which He swore to your fathers, as it is this day.
>
> Deuteronomy 8:18 (NKJV)

God wants to establish his covenant. What does that mean? In the book of Genesis, God promised that the entire world would be blessed through Abraham and his descendants. That was really a prophecy about God sending his Son, Jesus, into the world to save all of us from a life of hopelessness and failure. God wants us to take the gospel (good news) of Jesus Christ into the world, and to do that we need the resources. There is nowhere in the Bible that God wants his true followers to be religious and poor. God wants us to be blessed and fruitful.

> Let the LORD be magnified, who has pleasure in the prosperity of His servant.
>
> Psalm 35:27 (NKJV)

God enjoys it when you do well. It gives him pleasure. I truly believe that he has blessed our entire culture because of the faithfulness of his followers.

Conclusion

Now I'm sure that nothing I have written so far will convince you that the Bible is the Word of God if you don't want to believe it. To be perfectly frank, there is no scientific proof that the Bible is anything more than a collection of ancient writings. Then again, there is no scientific proof that it's anything less than Word of God, either. I believe that if you are willing to step out in faith and accept the Bible at face value, believe in its teachings, and apply its guiding principles to your life, you will see such incredible changes in your life that any doubts you might have would disappear forever. That being said, I want you to know that the Bible is the only basis for the rest of this book. All of the points I will make from this point forward will be based solely on the teachings of God's Word.

An Amazing God

> In the beginning God created the heavens and the earth.
>
> Genesis 1:1 (NLT)

Principle 2 – As Christians we believe that God, as he has revealed himself to us in his Word, is the sole authority and has complete control over everything that happens, not only on earth, but in the entire universe.

Several years ago I had a boss who, when we employees would question why or how we were doing something, would say, "You just don't understand the big picture." That is how it is with God; only he has the view of a much bigger picture than my boss had. It's an even bigger view than that of a mayor, a governor, or the president of the United States. God looks at things from the view of eternity, and his understanding is unlimited. It might seem like an impossible task for limited beings like us to try to understand an unlimited being like God, but he has revealed a few things about himself to us. He did it in his Word, the Bible. So if we haven't read the Bible, then it's no wonder we don't know anything about

God. We are left to speculation and the opinions of others. We might even come to the conclusion that God doesn't exist at all, which I am sure makes him sad, since he went to all the trouble to send us a letter (the Bible) to tell us all about himself.

Many people question the existence of God because modern scientific understanding seemingly contradicts the biblical account of creation given to us in the book of Genesis. The thing is, our limited understanding doesn't explain away God. Remember he has the big picture, and he understands how it all fits together. He created it all, and he has control over all of it.

> Let every soul be subject to the governing authorities. For there is no authority except from God, and the authorities that exist are appointed by God.
>
> Romans 13:1 (NKJV)

God is the final authority on everything. Anyone who has any authority on earth has either had that authority delegated to him directly by God, or God has allowed him to have that authority. That verse gives us a little command also. It says to be subject to the governing authorities. Sometimes we have real authority issues, and we don't like people telling us what to do. Here we see that God himself is the one who put those people in authority over us. Maybe you can consider them to be a test in your life, to see if you can learn to submit to authority even if it might not be right. You shouldn't have to do illegal or immoral things, but you can do things you disagree with, even if you think they might be off base or even kind of ignorant. In the Bible there are many stories of people who willingly submitted to the authority of another, even though it seemed unfair and unjust; but God rewarded the strength of their character, and they went on to accomplish great things in their own right.

Everything God wanted to reveal to us about himself is in the Bible. Any information you find about God that comes from any other source should be considered untrustworthy at best and downright wrong or a lie in the worst case. Here is what the Bible says about God:

God Revealed His Nature to Us through His Names

In the original languages of the Bible, the names used when talking about God have a special meaning and hold a specific purpose for their usage. Below are the Hebrew names for God. In parentheses you will see how the names are pronounced (at least to the best of my knowledge). Next you will see the way it is translated in English Bibles, followed by a brief definition, and finally a verse in the Bible where it is used. The parentheses in the Bible verses show the words that are actually used in the English Bibles.

Elohim (El-o-heem)

Translated in the Bible as *God,* Elohim means the supreme God, the powerful being that created the heavens and the earth. The interesting thing is that this is the plural form of the Hebrew word that means God (*El*). We'll talk about why that is a little bit later.

> Then Elohim [God] looked over all he had made, and he saw that it was very good!
>
> Genesis 1:31 (NLT)

Yahweh (Yaw-way)

Translated in the Bible as *the Lord,* (in small caps) Yahweh is an English attempt to pronounce a name that is unpronounceable. This word is actually God's name, and it means "the self-existent and eternal God." In other words, he exists. He always has, and he always will. He was not created by anyone. The challenge with this word is that in the Jewish faith this word is not to be spoken out loud. No one actually knows how it is pronounced because it is not pronounced. They simply call it "The Name." In public services they often substitute the word "Adonai" in its place. In ancient manuscripts God's name consists of four Hebrew consonants, Yud-Heh-Vav-Heh. It is written, YHVH. When William Tyndale was originally translating the Old Testament into English, he took the vowel sounds from *Adonai,* the word used in the Jewish religion, and combined them with the Hebrew consonants and coined the word *Jehovah.* Modern theologians think that *Yahweh* is probably a closer pronunciation.

> When everything was ready, Yahweh [the Lord] said to Noah, "Go into the boat with all your family, for among all the people of the earth, I can see that you alone are righteous."
>
> Genesis 7:1 (NLT)

The way *Yahweh* and *Elohim* are used together throughout the Old Testament really establishes that *Yahweh* is God's name. It is a concept I think we miss in our English translations of the Bible.

> This is what Yahweh [the LORD] the Elohim [God] of the Hebrews says, "Let my people go."
>
> Exodus 5:1 (NLT)

> Hear, O Israel: Yahweh [the LORD] our Elohim [God], Yahweh [the LORD] is one!
>
> Deuteronomy 6:4 (NKJV)

> Look today I am giving you a choice between a blessing and a curse. You will be blessed if you obey the commands of Yahweh [the LORD] your Elohim [God] that I am giving you today.
>
> Deuteronomy 11:26 (NLT)

> This is my command: "Be strong and courageous! Do not be afraid or discouraged for Yahweh [the LORD] your Elohim [God] is with you wherever you go."
>
> Joshua 1:9 (NLT)

> "How Foolish!" Samuel exclaimed, "You have not kept the command Yahweh [the LORD] your Elohim [God] gave you. If you kept it, Yahweh [the LORD] would have established your kingdom over Israel forever. But now your kingdom must end, for Yahweh [the LORD] has sought out a man after His own heart."
>
> 1 Samuel 13:13,14 (NLT)

> And Yahweh-Elohim [the Lord God] said, "It is not good for the man to be alone. I will make a helper who is just right for him."
>
> Genesis 2:18 (NLT)

El

The Hebrew word for God. It is usually used in combination with another word to give it its meaning. The most common one is the one we have been talking about, Elohim, the plural form of the creator God.

Here are some others:

1. *El-Shaddai (El-Shad-die).* Translated in the Bible as "the Almighty God" or "God-Almighty" depending on the translation. It means the powerful God who is sufficient to meet all of the needs of his people.

   > When Abram was ninety-nine years old, the Lord appeared to Abram and said to him, "I am El-Shaddai [Almighty God]; walk before me and be blameless."
   >
   > Genesis 17:1 (NKJV)

2. *El-Elyon (El-el-yawn).* Translated in the Bible as *God Most High.* It means the very highest God.

   > Melchizedek blessed Abram with this blessing: "Blessed be Abram by El-Elyon [God Most High], Creator of heaven and earth. And blessed be El-Elyon [God Most High], who has defeated your enemies for you."
   >
   > Genesis 14:19–20 (NLT)

3. *El-Olam (El-o-lam).* Translated in the Bible as the *eternal God.* It means the God that will live forever with no beginning and no end.

> Then Abraham planted a tamarisk tree at Beer-sheba, and there he worshiped Yahweh [the Lord], El-Olam [the Eternal God].
>
> Genesis 21:33 (NLT)

Adonai (Ad-o-ni)

Translated in the Bible as *Lord,* it means the *Sovereign Lord* or the one who doesn't have to answer to anyone. He makes decisions on his own and is accountable to no one.

> "Adonai [My Lord]," he said, "if it pleases you, stop here for a while."
>
> Genesis 18:3 (NLT)

Theos (Thee-aws)

This is the Greek word for God used in the New Testament. It is the Greek version of the Hebrew word *El.* It means the Supreme Creator God. It appears throughout the New Testament and is translated *God.* It is where we get the word *theology,* which means the study of God.

What have we learned from these names of God used in the Bible? We found out that he is the very highest and most powerful being in existence. He has no beginning and will have no end. He was not created by anyone, and he answers to no one.

God Revealed His Nature to Us through His Attributes

Throughout the Bible there are words and verses that describe what God is like. We call these his attributes or strengths. Here you will find some of his attributes listed. If needed a definition will be given, followed by a Bible verse where it is used, and then an explanation of what it means.

God is a Spirit.

> For God is Spirit, so those who worship Him must worship in spirit and in truth.
>
> John 4:24 (NKJV)

There is a place that actually exists called the spirit world. It is not some hazy, shadowy existence; it is an actual, authentic, and very real place. Maybe we could understand it as another dimension like something we might see on the Sci-Fi Channel. Paul, the apostle, writing in the New Testament about how we see the spiritual world, says it is like looking into a cloudy mirror. We can make out some forms and shapes, but we can't really comprehend what we are seeing.

We like to say that we will believe it when we see it, but we can only see the physical world around us. Here in the physical world, we can be fooled, and things are not always what they seem. However, there are no illusions in the spiritual world; everything is very real. Here on earth we are required to live by faith. Jesus told us, "Blessed are those that have not seen, yet still believe" (John 20:29, NKJV). In the spiritual world no faith is required because the reality of everything is laid out right before you. This is the world God exists in, and it is where the angels are. It is also where Satan and his demonic forces live.

We as human beings also have a spirit, and when we are born again we have a connection with that spirit world. We still don't fully understand it; but we have a connection to God, and he can reveal things to our spirit that we could never comprehend or believe otherwise. The Bible also says that our soul and spirit are eternal and after our time here on earth is over, we will go to a place where we will be able to understand it all. In the verse where Paul talked about the cloudy mirror, he also promised us that when that time comes, we will be able to see it all clearly and understand everything.

> Now we see things imperfectly as in a cloudy mirror, but then we will see everything with perfect clarity. All that I know now is partial and incomplete, but then I will know everything completely.
>
> 1 Corinthians 13:12 (NLT)

God is Infinite.

He is not limited by time or space. He has no beginning and will have no end.

1. He is infinite in relation to space.

> But will God indeed dwell on the earth? Behold, heaven and the heaven of heavens cannot contain You. How much less this temple which I have built!
>
> 1 Kings 8:27 (NKJV)

2. He is infinite in relation to time.

> Before the mountains were born, before you gave birth to the earth and the world, from beginning to end, you are God.
>
> Psalm 90:2 (NLT)

God is really beyond our human comprehension. He is not limited by time or space. Infinite means never ending. He goes on forever. From here on our tiny planet called Earth to beyond the very edges of the universe. From before the beginning of time to a time that never ends. Since we are finite, we can only be in one place and at one time. How can our puny little brains ever comprehend this infinite God?

God is Omnipotent.

Omni (all, absolutely, completely), potent (power or powerful). He is absolutely and completely powerful.

> O Sovereign Lord! You made the heavens and earth by your strong hand and powerful arm. Nothing is too hard for you!
>
> Jeremiah 32:17 (NLT)

God has the power to do whatever he wants to do, however he wants to do it, and whenever he wants to. The Bible says he spoke the universe into existence with only the power of his words. Then he formed human beings with his bare hands and breathed life into them. He will only use his power to do things that are within his character. As we go through these attributes, watch to see what kind of character God has, and then you will understand what he uses his unlimited power for.

God is Omnipresent.

Omni (all, absolutely, completely, everywhere), present (location, position). He is absolutely and completely located and positioned everywhere.

> I can never escape from your spirit! I can never get away from your presence! If I go up to heaven, you are there; if I go down to the place of the dead, you are there. If I ride the wings of the morning, if I dwell by the farthest oceans, even there your hand will guide me, and your strength will support me.
>
> Psalm 139:7–10 (NLT)

God is everywhere, all the time. So if a mother is praying for her child in South America, God is there. If a soldier in the Middle East is praying for God's protection, God is there. If someone in Asia finds out about God and cries out for salvation, God is there. If you, wherever you are right now, pray to God about anything, he is right there with you.

God is Omniscient.

Omni (all, absolutely, completely, everything), scient (science, knowledge). He absolutely and completely knows everything about everything. He is all knowledge.

> He counts the stars and calls them all by name. How great is our Lord! His power is absolute! His understanding is beyond comprehension!
>
> Psalm 147:4–5 (NLT)

God knows everything. He understands physics better than your physics teacher. He knows more about math than your math teacher. He also knows more about science, history, psychology, and music. He knows more about agriculture, medicine, and technology. He knows more about you than you know about yourself. The Bible says that even the hairs on your head are numbered. If you need to know something or you need to find something, why not ask God? He really does know everything.

God is Wise.

Wisdom is applied knowledge.

> But God made the earth by his power, and he preserves it by his wisdom. With his own understanding he stretched out the heavens.
>
> Jeremiah 10:12 (NLT)

> Christ is the mighty power of God and the wonderful wisdom of God. This "foolish" plan of God is far wiser than the wisest of human plans, and God's weakness is far stronger than the greatest of human strength.
>
> 1 Corinthians 1:24–25 (NLT)

This is a combination of his power and his knowledge. Since he has the power to do whatever he wants to and the knowledge of everything, then he also knows what to do and when to do it. Here is where we can learn to have faith and trust God. If he truly does have all of the knowledge and all of the power, then we can trust he also has the wisdom to know what is right for our lives. There are many things that happen in this world and even in our own lives (a fire, an accident, a death, etc.) that we don't understand. I believe that when we get to heaven and ask God about it, he will be able to explain it all to us.

God is Sovereign.

One who doesn't have to answer to anyone. He makes decisions on his own and is accountable to no one.

> He does according to His will in the army of heaven and among the inhabitants of the earth. No one can restrain His hand or say to Him, "What have You done?"
>
> Daniel 4:35 (NKJV)

God is the final authority on whatever takes place. There is no one who can challenge him or question him. He does not feel threatened by our doubts and objections.

God is Holy.

Holiness is absolute moral purity. God can neither sin nor tolerate sin.

> For I am the LORD who brings you up out of the land of Egypt, to be your God. You shall therefore be holy, for I am holy.
>
> Leviticus 11:45 (NLT)

God is absolutely ethical and has no hidden agendas. His motives are always pure, and he has complete integrity. He does not steal, he does not lie, and he does not cheat. He will never tell you one thing and do another. And then he asks us to do the same. Who can live up to that? No wonder the book of Romans says that we all fall short.

God is Righteous.

He always makes the right choices.

> The LORD is righteous in everything he does; he is filled with kindness.
>
> Psalm 145:17 (NLT)

God always makes the right choices, and he never makes mistakes. It is holiness in action. Holiness is his attitude toward everything, and righteousness is his actions based on those attitudes. We tend to think of those words as somehow being religious words, but they really aren't. God doesn't want us be pious and have a holier-than-thou attitude; he wants us to have a high moral character, make good choices, and live a good life. Of course, as I said, we all fall short of that, but God is always there to forgive us when we mess up and there to help us get back on the right track.

God is Merciful.

> The LORD is merciful and gracious; he is slow to get angry and full of unfailing love. He will not constantly accuse us, nor remain angry forever. He has not punished us for all our sins, nor does he deal with us as we deserve. For his unfailing love toward those who fear him is as great as the height of the heavens above the earth. He has removed our rebellious acts as far away from us as the east is from the west.
>
> Psalm 103:8–12 (NLT)

When we seek forgiveness, he is faithful to forgive us. The Newsboys sing a song that sums up God's grace and mercy quite well: *"When we don't get what we deserve, that's a real good thing. When we get what we don't deserve, that's a real good thing."*[3]

God lets us off the hook for our disobedient and rebellious actions. He allows us to receive blessings that we did nothing to earn. Did you notice that verse says, "your rebellious ways are removed as far as the east is from the west," not "as far as the north is from the south?" That speaks of forever. If you go north far enough, you will cross over the North Pole and begin to go south. If you continue south you will eventually cross the South Pole and start north. You can go east forever never reaching the end, and it is the same for going west; they never meet. Do you think that God might have known the world was round a long time before people figured it out?

God is Faithful.

He is absolutely trustworthy. He can never go back on his Word. His Word will never fail.

> But the Lord is faithful; he will make you strong and guard you from the evil one.
>
> 2 Thessalonians 3:3 (NLT)

There are many promises and many prophecies in the Word of God. God is so faithful that every one of them will come true. It is an absolute guarantee. Nothing in this world comes close to him. He is totally reliable. If God said it, it will happen. You can count on it.

God is Love.

God doesn't just love; he is the embodiment of love. He is love.

> Beloved, let us love one another, for love is of God; and everyone who loves is born of God and knows God. He who does not love does not know God, for *God is love.*
>
> 1 John 4:7–8 (NKJV)

> Who shall separate us from the love of Christ? Shall tribulation, or distress, or persecution, or famine, or nakedness, or peril, or sword? Yet in all these things we are more than conquerors through Him who loved us. For I am persuaded that neither death nor life, nor angels nor principalities nor powers, nor things present nor things to come, nor height nor depth, nor any other created thing, shall be able to separate us from the love of God which is in Christ Jesus our Lord.
>
> Romans 8:35, 37–39 (NKJV)

Most people have a real misperception of God. They think he is some mean old guy with a long beard watching us from up in the sky, just waiting for us to mess up so he can reach down and beat us over the head with a stick. They think he put all these impossible rules in place just to keep us from having any fun.

The truth is, God loves you with an indescribable love. If you have children, think of how much you love your kids and multiply that by a million. You would still not come close to how much God loves you. It doesn't matter what you've done, where you've been, or what has happened to you. Your past and your actions are totally irrelevant to God's love. He loves you completely, totally, and unconditionally.

God is Good.

Every good thing in this world comes from God. Every bad thing does not come from God.

> The LORD is good, a strong refuge when trouble comes. He is close to those who trust in him.
>
> Nahum 1:7 (NLT)

> Whatever is good and perfect comes down to us from God our Father, who created all the lights in the heavens. He never changes or casts a shifting shadow. He chose to give birth to us by giving us his true word. And we, out of all creation, became his prized possession.
>
> James 1:17–18 (NLT)

> For I know the thoughts that I think toward you, says the LORD, thoughts of peace and not of evil, to give you a future and a hope.
>
> Jeremiah 29:11 (NKJV)

This goes along with the previous point. God is good, and he has only your very best interests in mind. A lot of very bad things happen in this world, and God gets blamed for most all of them. Over the next few chapters we will learn where most of that bad stuff comes from and find that God did not have anything to do with it at all.

The Trinity–Three Individual Persons in One Godhead

This is the last point I want to make about God, and it is probably the most difficult. Most of us have heard of God the Father, God the Son, and God the Holy Spirit. We hear their names at baptisms and weddings and other religious gatherings, but do we have any idea what it means or how it could even be? There is only one God, but there are three distinct persons in the Godhead. This is very difficult to understand and even more difficult to explain. I told you early in this chapter that God is an infinite God and we are finite human beings, so the very idea that we could comprehend God is actually pretty unreasonable. Even my computer just told me I was messing up. It told me I have a numbering problem in the very first sentence of this paragraph and that I should "consider revising." Three in one is just not possible. The best way to take this point is to just believe it, don't try to totally comprehend it. That being said, let's look at some of the places where the concept of a trinity does show up in the Bible.

The Most Common Hebrew Word used for God is a Plural Word.

Remember Elohim, the Creator God, the first of God's names that we talked about? We said that it is the plural form of the Hebrew word for God (*El*). So *Elohim* means more than one.

> In the beginning Elohim [God] created the heavens and the earth.
>
> Genesis 1:1 (NKJV)

> Hear, O Israel: Yahweh [the LORD] our Elohim [God], Yahweh [the LORD] is one!
>
> Deuteronomy 6:4 (NKJV)

Here we see that Yahweh is our Elohim, which is plural, but Yahweh is one.

To Whom Was God Talking?

> Then Elohim (God) said, "Let Us make man in Our image, according to Our likeness."
>
> Genesis 1:26 (NKJV)

We know he hadn't created man yet. And as we will find out in the next couple of chapters, we were not made in the image of angels, so who was he talking to when he referred to himself as "us"? I think it is only logical to believe the Father was talking to the Son and the Holy Spirit.

A Time When They Were All Named Together

There is an event in the Bible where the Father, the Son, and the Holy Spirit were all mentioned as being together in the same place at the same time. It happened at the baptism of Jesus.

> When He had been baptized, Jesus came up immediately from the water; and behold, the heavens were opened to Him, and He saw the Spirit of God descending like a dove and alighting upon

> Him. And suddenly a voice came from heaven, saying, "This is My beloved Son, in whom I am well pleased."
>
> Matthew 3:16–17 (NKJV)

So here we see the Son (Jesus) being baptized in the Jordan River. After he came up out of the water, the Holy Spirit, in the form of a dove, flew down out of heaven and landed on him. Then a voice from heaven, the Father, said, "This is my beloved Son, in whom I am well pleased." This is the only place in the Bible where it is spelled out that all three of them were in the same place at the same time.

They All Have the Same Attributes

We just listed some of the many attributes of God. There are verses in the Bible that refer to each of the persons of the Godhead (the Father, the Son, and the Holy Spirit) as having each of those attributes. So the Holy Spirit is infinite, omnipresent, omnipotent, wise, sovereign, etc. And Jesus has them all as well. So as you read through that list, know that they all apply to all three of them.

Conclusion

If you don't remember any of the other points in this chapter, remember the last two of the attributes. God is good, and he loves you very much. Some bad things may have happened to you in your past; but God did not do it, and he is there to rescue you if you ask him. Pray right now for God to reveal himself to you through the rest of these chapters as you read them. And ask him how you can put these principles into practice in your own life so you can begin to experience God's goodness and God's love for you.

God's Special Creation

> Then God said, "Let Us make man in Our image, according to Our likeness; let them have dominion over the fish of the sea, over the birds of the air, and over the cattle, over all the earth and over every creeping thing that creeps on the earth." So God created man in His own image; in the image of God He created him; male and female He created them.
>
> Genesis 1:26–27 (NKJV)

Principle 3 – As Christians we believe that humans were created in the image of God, to have a special relationship with God, and with a purpose and a destiny that can only be fulfilled by living in obedience to God's Word and by following his direction for our lives.

And the LORD God formed man of the dust of the ground, and breathed into his nostrils the breath of life; and man became a living being.

Genesis 2:7 (NKJV)

And the LORD God caused a deep sleep to fall on Adam, and he slept; and He took one of his ribs, and closed up the flesh in its place. Then the rib

> which the LORD God had taken from man He made into a woman, and He brought her to the man.
>
> Genesis 2:26–27 (NKJV)

God created mankind. We aren't an accident of nature. We weren't the result of a big bang. We aren't descended from ape-like creatures that lived millions of years ago. We are an amazing creation, very dear to the heart of God. In this chapter we will look at what makes you so special and what sets you apart from the rest of creation.

God's Image in Man

Three in One

At the end of the last chapter, we discussed how God is three persons in one. He created us that way too. As human beings we have three parts: our spirit, our soul, and our body.

1. *Our spirit.* In Genesis 2:7 above, it says that God breathed into man the breath of life. That breath of life is our spirit. It is our source of life, and it is what separates us from the animal kingdom. It is kind of hard for us to define because as we mentioned in the last chapter, we can see, touch,

smell, taste, and hear the physical world, but our understanding of the spiritual world is very limited. We were created by God to have a relationship with God. That relationship is the only reason we exist at all, and our spirit is where that relationship takes place. It is our connection with the spirit world God lives in. We were designed to stroll through life together with him. He wants us to have the kind of relationship where we love to spend time together, where we communicate and share our lives with each other. Sounds a lot like marriage, doesn't it? As a matter of fact, that is a very common metaphor used in the Bible for our relationship with God. God longs to have that kind of relationship with each of us.

2. *Our soul.* We tend to think of our soul and our spirit as different terms for the same thing. Actually they are quite different. Our soul is who we are. It is where our thinking takes place and where our emotions and willpower are located. It is where our personality is. It is who we are when no one is looking. It was placed within us by God when we were created, then develops throughout our lifetime. It determines how we react to the world around us and how the world reacts to us. It is where we make our choices and decisions.

3. *Our body.* Our spirit, soul, and body all come into existence at the same moment, inside of our mother's womb. Our spirit and soul together are known as our inner man, and they will last forever, from the point of our conception on. Our physi-

cal body, however, will only last until our life on earth is over. It is the house we live in on our walk through life. We tend to think of it as who we are, and we make decisions on what we think of other people by the appearance of their body. But actually it is only temporary and has very little to do with who we really are. That's why the Bible says: "For the LORD does not see as man sees; for man looks at the outward appearance, but the LORD looks at the heart [spirit and soul]" (1 Samuel 16:7, NKJV).

Our body is an amazing piece of machinery though. I really don't understand how someone could look at a human body and think it somehow came into existence by accident or that it somehow evolved from a lower form of life. Think about how your eyeballs work to give you sight or your ears to give you hearing. Think about your digestive system, your circulatory system, your nervous system, and your reproductive system. All of them are placed within a structure of bones, tendons, muscles, and flesh. What an amazing creation you truly are.

A Desire for a Spiritual Connection with God

Because we are spiritual beings, we have an intense desire for spiritual things. Since we live in a physical world and in a culture that denies the supernatural, we don't always realize what that desire is. But this is the underlying reason we have so many religions in the world; why we call the psychic hotline, visit fortunetellers, and read our horoscope; why movies, TV shows, and games about the spirit world and the paranormal are so popular.

Moral Character

We all have something deep inside of us that somehow knows the difference between right and wrong. We have a sense of justice that causes us to get angry when we see the innocent hurt or taken advantage of. If we do something that violates our sense of right and wrong or our sense of justice, we feel guilty. God is the one who placed that within us, and it is what separates us from the rest of creation. Have you ever met a tiger with a guilty conscience? You will probably never hear an elephant say, *"I need to be better elephant."* But I bet you've heard a man say, *"I need to be a better dad."* Animals were designed to live by instinct, and they will only act the way they were designed to act. We, on the other hand, can make a decision to change, to be better, not to make some of the bad choices that have caused us such difficulty in the past.

Reason

Along that same line, we have the ability to understand, to discover, and to gain knowledge. We can solve math and science problems or figure out how to arrange the furniture in our house. We can learn from experience, and as was just mentioned, we can learn to make better choices. Some animals have a limited ability to learn and can even experience some degree of behavior modification. But we as humans have the ability to completely change our lifestyle if we decide to. We can move to a different city or even country. We can change jobs, we can change families, and we can even change the way we look.

Our Instincts

God also placed within us some special driving forces (instincts) to help us survive on planet Earth.

Self-preservation. This is the number-one driving force in our lives. All of the others are there to support this one. We will do whatever it takes to survive. We have a special mechanism built inside of us called "fight or flight." When we sense harm, we will run away if we have the opportunity or fight back with whatever means we have at our disposal if we have no other choice. If we have some special skills or experience, some of us may be more willing to stand and fight than others.

Gathering. We like to have possessions, something that belongs to just us. You can see it in children. They are always looking at things they see on TV and thinking, *I need that!* If you were to give a doll to a little girl or a toy truck to a boy in a third-world country, it would become their most valued treasure. Our ancestors would acquire items for their tents or caves. Women liked to look for things to make themselves more beautiful and their homes a pleasant place to live in. Men wanted to look for tools and weapons to feed and protect their families. We haven't changed much, have we? You ladies love jewelry, shoes, pretty clothes, and items to make your homes beautiful. We men, a little less concerned with clothes, shoes, and how the house looks, still love tools, weapons, and we like our toys too, like golf clubs, trucks, computers, and boats.

Food and water. This is a rather obvious one. We all know we need to eat and will die without water. It is a very serious drive all of us have. We will do whatever it takes to find something to eat and something to drink. People in third-world countries will go through the city dumps looking for scraps. The homeless and impoverished in our own cities might go through dumpsters and garbage cans looking for the same. People will cheat and steal to feed themselves and their families. It is what we go to work for every day, "to put bread on the table."

Reproduction. Did you know that God gave you that sex drive? Sigmund Freud thought he made some great discovery when he said we were all motivated by our sexual urges. Duh? God gave you that! It is described in the very first chapter of the Bible.

> Then God blessed them, and said to them, "Be fruitful and multiply; fill the earth and subdue it; have dominion over the fish of the sea, over the birds of the air, and over every living thing that moves on the earth."
>
> Genesis 1:28–29 (NKJV)

How were we going to be fruitful and multiply and fill the earth without a drive for sex? God not only approves of sex; he designed it!

> Therefore a man shall leave his father and mother and be joined to his wife, and they shall become one flesh.
>
> Genesis 2:24 (NKJV)

This is such an important verse that Jesus quoted it. It's recorded in the books of Matthew and Mark. Then the Apostle Paul quoted it again in the book of Ephesians. God wants a man to be "joined" to his wife. That word is translated "cling to his wife" in the King James Version. It means to be tightly adhered to, to be firmly and permanently attached. The very word itself has a sexual connotation and also has a meaning of face to face. God designed the sexual relationship between a husband and a wife to be enjoyable, fulfilling, and permanent. In God's plan, a young man and a young woman who were still virgins would get married, stay faithful to each other throughout their marriage, and have a fulfilling sexual relationship that lasted a lifetime. How many problems would that eliminate from our society if we all lived by God's design? That also sets you apart from the rest of creation. Animals mate by instinct; enjoyment, fulfillment, and commitment have nothing to do with it. I'm glad God had a better plan for humans.

Now I know that in our modern culture very few of us live up to that level of purity, but God also told us that when we become Christians: "Therefore, if anyone *is* in Christ, *he is* a new creation; old things have passed away; behold, all things have become new" 2 Corinthians 5:17 (NKJV). That means that when we accept Jesus we get to start all over and begin a new life as pure as if we were a brand new baby.

Dominance. God even commanded us to have dominion over the earth. When we see that word, *dominion*, we think of the word dominate. To most of us, that has the negative implication of exploitation and abuse. What it really means is the ability to use the resources. We as humans have the ability to use this planet Earth to help us survive. We can plant crops and harvest the grains, vegetables, and fruits we need to live on. We can dam rivers to use for energy and to irrigate our crops. We can chop down trees and use them to build our homes and businesses. We can mine metals from the ground and use them to make our cars, planes, and ships, and we can pump oil from deep in the earth to fuel them. God expects us to use our ability to reason and our moral character to be wise and responsible with our dominion of the earth.

Our Individual Temperaments

We have learned how God made all of us as human beings, but he also created each of us completely unique. He has a plan and a purpose for each of us to complete in our lifetime on planet Earth. In order for us to accomplish this special assignment he has for us, we each have unique gifts and talents that only we possess. Here are some verses in the Bible that talk about our specialness and our uniqueness.

For You formed my inward parts;
You covered me in my mother's womb.
I will praise You, for I am fearfully and wonderfully made;
Marvelous are Your works,
And that my soul knows very well.
My frame was not hidden from You,
When I was made in secret,
And skillfully wrought in the lowest parts of the earth.
Your eyes saw my substance, being yet unformed.
And in Your book they all were written,
The days fashioned for me,
When as yet there were none of them.

Psalm 139:13–16 (NKJV)

The LORD gave me this message: "I knew you before I formed you in your mother's womb. Before you were born I set you apart and appointed you as my prophet to the nations."

Jeremiah 1:4–5 (NLT)

God has given each of us the ability to do certain things well. So if God has given you the ability to prophesy, speak out when you have faith that God is speaking through you. If your gift is that of serving others, serve them well. If you are a teacher, do a good job of teaching. If your gift is to encourage others, do it! If you have money, share it generously. If God has given you leadership ability, take the responsibility seriously. And if you have a gift for showing kindness to others, do it gladly. Don't just pretend that you love others. Really love them. Hate what is wrong. Stand on the side of the good. Love each other with genuine affection, and

> take delight in honoring each other. Never be lazy in your work, but serve the Lord enthusiastically. Be glad for all God is planning for you.
>
> Romans 12:6–12 (NLT)

God looked down through the eons of time to this place in this time and placed you right here, right now. You were not an accident. It doesn't matter what your parents were thinking. God knew and God planned it. All of our circumstances are not perfect; as a matter of fact some of them are very difficult. But God still has a plan; he has a specific purpose for you. A role that only you, in all of your uniqueness, can fulfill.

Your environment growing up has had a huge impact on who you are, whether it was good or bad: the input you had from your parents, grandparents, uncles, aunts, cousins, and friends; your teachers, coaches, and church leaders; your city, state, area of the county, and your own neighborhood; your race, culture, and religion. All of these helped determine who you are today. You could also be affected by a particular traumatic event like a death in the family, a rape, a fire, an automobile accident, or moving across the country or around the world. We have all had very unique circumstances in our lives that have influenced how we turned out.

God put something inside of you that has probably had the biggest impact on who you are. It is called your temperament. It was placed within you by God while you were developing in your mother's womb, as King David wrote in the verse we just read from Psalm 136. Your temperament determines how you react to the events and people around you, and it determines how they react to you.

The study of temperaments or personalities goes back as far as history itself. Hippocrates[4] who lived in ancient Greece from 460 to 370 b.c., was the first to document the names of four different temperament types. The Greeks' theory of human body function and how they came up with these words has proven to be misguided by modern science, but we still use his terminology. As we go through these, see if you can recognize yourself. Very few of us are pure temperament types like these listed; we usually have a blend of them that helps make us all unique.

Melancholy. People with this temperament tend to be quiet and probably introverted; they might struggle with their self-esteem. They tend to be very perfectionistic and detail oriented. They like things organized and in order. If you were to look in their cupboards, drawers, closets, or their garages, you would see their clothes folded or hung neatly and spaced perfectly, with everything organized by color and style; their dishes and silverware perfectly organized; and their tools cleaned and meticulously put away where they belong. Things that are messy or out of place really drive them crazy. So if your messiness really gets on the nerves of someone you know or love, you might be dealing with a Melancholy. They will probably excel at tedious work that requires precision and accuracy, and they prefer to work alone and not have to deal with people. They also tend to be creative and innovative. Many of the artists, musicians, and song writers in the world are Melancholy. They are also thinkers. They will look at every side of an issue before making a decision. They hate to be impulsive.

Choleric. These are the leaders, the movers, and the shakers. They want to be in charge. They love to be in charge. They have to be in charge. They have the ability to motivate people and influence people to accomplish what they want to see accomplished. They always have the best idea, at least in their opinion, of how things need to be done. They think, *you can go ahead and do things your way if you want to be wrong, but it would be more efficient and much wiser on your part if you would just go along with me and quit being so stubborn.* The world needs these kinds of leaders. There are not very many of us willing to stand up, take the lead, and get things done. Most of us would prefer to sit in the background and second-guess the leaders but are not willing to step up and take charge. The Cholerics are perfectly willing and able.

Sanguine. These are the happy, cheerful people. They love to go where the action is. They always have places to go, people to see, and things to do. They like things loud and bright, and they love to be spontaneous. They enjoy going to the mall, to concerts, to parties, wherever they can find people and action. They tend to be lighthearted, and they love to tell jokes and stories. If their story needs a little embellishment or exaggeration to make it even better, that's okay; it might even be required. They are the life of the party, and they love to be the center of attention. They tend to be a little irresponsible, but we are willing to overlook it because they are so enjoyable to be around. We love having them as our friends because they are so much fun.

Phlegmatic. Balanced is the best way to describe a Phlegmatic. They tend to be calm and easygoing. It's hard to ruffle their feathers or get them upset about anything. It's also hard to get them thrilled or excited about anything. They tend to go through life on an even keel without too many extreme highs or extreme lows. They are practical, down-to-earth people and are usually very pleasant to be around; they will rarely have emotional or angry outbursts. They are normally very patient, efficient, and slightly perfectionistic. They will probably excel at jobs that involve numbers and details.

This also can be a balancer for the extremes of the other temperaments. For example if a person is a Sanguine-Phlegmatic, he could have the same cheerful personality as a pure Sanguine without the extreme drive to be a party animal. A Melancholy-Phlegmatic might have the same detailed-oriented outlook as a pure Melancholy but wouldn't be quite so impatient with things not totally perfect.

Can you see yourself in any of these? Probably not to the extremes of some of them, but I'm sure you recognize the tendencies. Remember that most likely you have a blend of these different temperaments that makes you unique. And your unique temperament, combined with your unique circumstances of life, make you the only person just like you that has ever lived. You're a pretty amazing creation, aren't you?

Men and Women

One more way God added to our uniqueness is by making us men and women. This is probably the most dramatic difference of all.

We have some very obvious differences physically. On average:

- Men are usually larger and stronger than women.
- Forty percent of a man's body weight is muscle while a woman's is only twenty-three percent.
- Women have larger kidneys, liver, and stomach, but smaller lungs.
- Men have larger hands, a narrower face, longer legs, and a longer upper body.
- Women have a larger, more active thyroid. It expands during pregnancy and menstruation and is associated with smooth skin and a relatively hairless body, which are good things.

Those are only a few of our physical differences. There are many more, but you get the idea: we're different. Our emotional makeup, our way of thinking, and our view of the world are also quite different, in some ways, almost totally opposite. It is almost as if we are two completely different species.

It all starts long before we are even born. Sometime early in the pregnancy, God decided that little boys need to take a chemical bath. They are doused with testosterone and other sex-related hormones, and this soaking has a huge effect on the male brain. Some of the connecting fibers, called corpus collosum, between the two brain hemispheres are destroyed, and the gray matter of the brain shrinks slightly causing the white matter to expand. So you could say, as a lot of women have suspected all along, that men are basically brain damaged.

Why do you suppose God chose to do that to the little boys? Well, it caused us to have a special way of thinking that is quite different from how women think. Men are unilateral thinkers, so most of the time we only use one side of our brain at a time, and we are usually left-brain dominant. The left side of the brain is the analytical, logical, and factual side of the brain. We like to figure things out logically and have things spelled out for us in black and white.

Women are bilateral thinkers. They use both sides of their brain at the same time. The right side is where creativity takes place, where feelings and emotions reside, and it is the center for language and communication. So women are connected with these areas all of the time. Women are no less skilled at analytical, logical, factual thinking than men. It's just that in all of their thinking, the creativity, emotions, and communication are always present.

The white matter is the part of the brain where spatial reasoning takes place. Since in the male brain the gray matter shrunk slightly and the white matter expanded, most men are quite adept at understanding designs and shapes. This is the ability to read a blue print and understand what the building will look like when it is finished, to be able to look at a room and figure out what needs to be done and how the room will look after it is remodeled and fixed up, to have the ability to take some wooden boards, do a little trimming, cutting, sanding, and shaping and come out with a beautiful piece of furniture.

The gray matter is the part of the brain where the real heavy-duty thinking, calculating, and figuring takes place. Since the women don't have to go through this chemical bath and lose any of their connections between the sides of their brain or the shrinkage of their gray matter, they seem to have some special abilities and advantages in these areas. They have quicker access to language and reasoning skills and can leave us males in the dust with their ability to rapidly read a situation, formulate an argument, and articulate a response. You women need to go easy on us guys, because in a war of wits we are normally unarmed and unprepared.

Because of how their brains work, men also have the unique ability to compartmentalize. We take all of the different areas of our lives and separate them into different boxes. Work, home, hobbies, sports, children, marriage, friends, projects, and however many other different things we can think of to get involved in—they will each have their own separate box. Many times we won't even comprehend that there is any connection between them. It also gives men a special ability to focus and block out distractions. Ladies, if you've ever tried to talk to a man while he's watching a football game, you know what I mean. Men like to go to easy boxes, places where they have had success and get good feedback. They do their best to avoid the difficult boxes.

On the other hand, for a woman everything is connected. Every piece of her life has everything to do with everything else. Bill and Pam Farrel wrote an excellent book describing this phenomenon called *Men Are Like Waffles and Women Are Like Spaghetti.*[5] It compares all of the little compartments that men have in their lives to the many little boxes on a waffle, and it relates the way women think to a plate full of spaghetti. Instead of separate compartments, each of the many areas of their lives is like a noodle, and all of their noodles are touching all of their other noodles. They are intertwined and wrapped around each other, so that every area of their life is connected with every other area. If a woman is having trouble with one of her noodles, it will affect all of her other noodles. She can't just avoid it as men do their difficult boxes.

Because of our different ways of thinking, men and women also approach life differently. Women were created to be relationship oriented, and they will always strive to please their families and also be pleased by their families. They will do things to make their homes clean and beautiful, they look for ways to save money, and they make purchases with someone in mind. They like weddings and family get-togethers. Since they are always thinking of their relationships with others, they are very good at buying gifts and cards to commemorate birthdays, anniversaries, and other special events. Their self-esteem is wrapped up in how well their families and marriages are doing.

Men are driven more by goals and accomplishments. Their self-esteem is built on the things they are able to achieve or not achieve with their lives. Family and relationships tend to fall further down the priority list and will take a backseat to the things they are trying to accomplish.

The thing you have to realize is that both men and women are created in the image of God. Neither is wrong or right, and neither is better or worse. They are just different, and that's God's plan. He gave each of us different roles and responsibilities in our homes. He gave men the role of provider and protector for his family, and he gave women the role of nourisher and comforter for her family. We can both go into the other's world and be as successful as we want to be, but we will only feel content and fulfilled if our primary role is being taken care of too.

Conclusion

We're a pretty remarkable creation, aren't we? So incredibly complex and intricately designed and still so marvelously unique. Created in the very image of God himself, with all of the instincts we need for survival yet so totally different that not any two of us are alike. You've got to wonder, though, if everything is so perfect and good, then why are we all so messed up? Why is my life such a wreck? And why is everyone around me so hard to get along with? Let's see if we can figure that out right now.

Our Fall from Grace

> You will be accepted if you respond in the right way. But if you refuse to respond correctly, then watch out! Sin is waiting to attack and destroy you, and you must subdue it.
>
> Genesis 4:6 (NLT)

Principle 4 – As Christians we believe that when sin became part of our human existence we were separated from God. Our relationship with him was severed, and we lost the opportunity to fulfill the purpose and the destiny he created us for.

> Then the LORD God planted a garden in Eden, in the east, and there he placed the man he had created. And the Lord God planted all sorts of trees in the garden—beautiful trees that produced delicious fruit. At the center of the garden he placed the tree of life and the tree of the knowledge of good and evil. The LORD God placed the man in the Garden of Eden to tend and care for it. But the LORD God gave him this warning: "You may freely eat any fruit in the garden except fruit from the tree of the knowledge of good and evil. If you eat of its fruit, you will surely die."
>
> Genesis 2:8–9, 15–17 (NLT)

Now the serpent was the shrewdest of all the creatures the LORD God had made.

“Really?” he asked the woman. “Did God really say you must not eat any of the fruit in the garden?”

“Of course we may eat it,” the woman told him. ”It’s only the fruit from the tree at the center of the garden that we are not allowed to eat. God says we must not eat it or even touch it, or we will die.”

“You won’t die!” the serpent hissed. ”God knows that your eyes will be opened when you eat it. You will become just like God, knowing everything, both good and evil.”

The woman was convinced. The fruit looked so fresh and delicious, and it would make her so wise! So she ate some of the fruit. She also gave some to her husband, who was with her. Then he ate it, too. At that moment, their eyes were opened, and they suddenly felt shame at their nakedness. So they strung fig leaves together around their hips to cover themselves.

Toward evening they heard the LORD God walking about in the garden, so they hid themselves among the trees. The LORD God called to Adam, “Where are you?”

He replied, “I heard you, so I hid. I was afraid because I was naked.”

“Who told you that you were naked?” the LORD God asked. “Have you eaten the fruit I commanded you not to eat?”

"Yes," Adam admitted, "but it was the woman you gave me who brought me the fruit, and I ate it."

Then the LORD God asked the woman, "How could you do such a thing?"

"The serpent tricked me," she replied. "That's why I ate it."

So the LORD God said to the serpent, "Because you have done this, you will be punished. You are singled out from all the domestic and wild animals of the whole earth to be cursed. You will grovel in the dust as long as you live, crawling along on your belly. From now on, you and the woman will be enemies, and your offspring and her offspring will be enemies. He will crush your head, and you will strike his heel."

Then he said to the woman, "You will bear children with intense pain and suffering. And though your desire will be for your husband, he will be your master."

And to Adam he said, "Because you listened to your wife and ate the fruit I told you not to eat, I have placed a curse on the ground. All your life you will struggle to scratch a living from it. It will grow thorns and thistles for you, though you will eat of its grains. All your life you will sweat to produce food, until your dying day. Then you will return to the ground from which you came. For you were made from dust, and to the dust you will return."

Genesis 3:1–19 (NLT)

It all began in the Garden of Eden. God gave Adam and Eve the entire world to do whatever they wanted with. They could go wherever they wanted, do whatever they wanted to do, and eat whatever they wanted to eat. But there was one tree in the center of the garden that they were not to eat from. It was called the Tree of the Knowledge of Good and Evil. Even though the fruit from every tree in the world was available to them, they still felt that they needed to find out what they were missing and eat from the tree they were forbidden to. Because of their choice, they were kicked out of the garden and separated from God. From that day forward, all of mankind, every single one of us, has been born separated from God.

Sin is part of our nature; it is who we are. We are born sinners, and there is nothing we can do about it. In this Western culture that we have been talking about, most of us are pretty self-sufficient and don't really see a need for God in our lives. But in all of our abilities and prosperity, we still can't restore that relationship with God that was destroyed in the Garden of Eden. And we can't get rid of the sin problem that troubles all of us.

In this chapter we will learn about sin and what it has done to us. First we will look at what sin is. Then we will discuss where it comes from and finally the effect sin has had on our lives.

What Is Sin?

Chata - Hebrew, translated *sin* in the Old Testament.

Hamartia - Greek, translated *sin* in the New Testament.

The most commonly used words in the Bible that are translated *sin* mean to miss the mark or to be off target. Sin is an archery term that means to miss the bull's-eye. When the Bible was translated into English, the writers chose a term from competition and war that they thought everyone would comprehend and be able to understand what it meant. Some modern alternatives might be *out of bounds, foul ball, incomplete pass, error,* or *fault.* Whatever our choice, it means we are out of sync with God's design and plans for our life.

If we were to shoot an arrow in an archery contest and our aim was just a fraction of an inch off, we would miss that bull's-eye. We might even miss the target all together. NASA scientists can launch a spacecraft into outer space with amazing accuracy. But if they were to have the tiniest discrepancy in their calculations of the spacecraft's direction, it could be off course by millions of miles by the time it reaches deep space. That's how our lives are. When we are at odds with God's purposes, we miss our target destination altogether.

Over the centuries since the Bible was translated into English, we have lost the original implication of that word *sin.* It has developed more of a religious meaning, and we tend to think of things we do wrong that the Bible tells us not to, like lying, cheating, or stealing. In reality, those things are just symptoms of a deeper problem, a life off target with God's desired direction for us. If our lives are out of sync with God, it will be revealed by our actions. All of our bad behavior and selfish actions are technically sin, but in reality it is our sinful nature going against God's holy nature and causing us to make bad choices.

Where Does Sin Come From?

> But each one is tempted when he is drawn away by his own desires and enticed. Then, when desire has conceived, it gives birth to sin; and sin, when it is full-grown, brings forth death.
>
> James 1:13–15 (NKJV)

Our Own Desires

We like to quote that great theologian Flip Wilson and say, "The devil made me do it!" For those of you not old enough to remember him, Flip was a popular comedian back in the 1970s, and that was one of his taglines. Satan does have a role to play in our sin, just as he did with Eve, and we'll get to that in a minute. The reality, though, is that sin comes from deep inside of us. That verse we just read states, "We are drawn away by our own desires."

We are born with a sinful nature, and we have the built-in ability to do wrong. If you have ever been around babies, you probably noticed that you didn't have to teach them how to be selfish or how to throw a little tantrum if they don't get their way. They come by it naturally. Even though they are adorable and precious, they still are all born with a sinful nature.

As we grow, it is still part of all of us. We are naturally dishonest, immoral, and selfish. Hopefully, over the course of our lifetime, our parents, our teachers, and others with influence over our lives have taught us how to behave ourselves and what appropriate public behavior is. We have been taught that lying, cheating, and stealing are not acceptable, but deep inside of us, when no one is looking, sin and bad choices are still part of our lives. Many people without good role models in their lives have never learned that bad behavior is unacceptable. Some, even with good role models and good training, have still allowed themselves to develop the bad habits and exhibit the bad behaviors that destroy lives. Whatever our life is like and however we have learned to behave, we all still have one thing in common: we are all sinners.

> For all have sinned; all fall short of God's glorious standard.
>
> Romans 3:23 (NLT)

The Enticement

This is where Satan comes in. His real name is Lucifer, and he used to be God's right hand man. He was called the Angel of Light, a beautiful creature that was created by God to be his minister of music. When God created humans, Lucifer was apparently jealous of man's unique place in God's heart. Remember in the last chapter we talked about how God created you in his own image to have a special relationship with him. Angels have a different role in God's kingdom. The word *angel* could also be translated as *messenger.* Lucifer was not satisfied with taking a back seat to this special human race that God created, and he rebelled against God. The rebellion is recorded in both the books of Isaiah and Ezekiel.

How you are fallen from heaven,
O Lucifer, son of the morning!
How you are cut down to the ground,
You who weakened the nations!
For you have said in your heart:
"I will ascend into heaven,
I will exalt my throne above the stars of God;
I will also sit on the mount of the congregation
On the farthest sides of the north;
I will ascend above the heights of the clouds,
I will be like the Most High."
Yet you shall be brought down to Sheol,
To the lowest depths of the Pit.
Isaiah 14:12–15 (NKJV)

Thus says the LORD GOD, "You were
the seal of perfection,
Full of wisdom and perfect in beauty.
You were in Eden, the garden of God;
Every precious stone was your covering: The sardius, topaz, and diamond, beryl, onyx, and jasper, sapphire, turquoise, and emerald with gold.
The workmanship of your timbrels and pipes was
prepared for you on the day you were created.
"You were the anointed cherub who covers; I established you;

You were on the holy mountain of God;
You walked back and forth in the midst of fiery stones.
You were perfect in your ways from
the day you were created,
Till iniquity was found in you.
"By the abundance of your trading you became
filled with violence within, and you sinned;
Therefore I cast you as a profane thing
out of the mountain of God;
And I destroyed you, O covering cherub,
From the midst of the fiery stones.
"Your heart was lifted up because of your beauty;
You corrupted your wisdom for the sake of your splendor;
I cast you to the ground, I laid you before kings,
That they might gaze at you.
"You defiled your sanctuaries by the multitude of your iniquities,
By the iniquity of your trading;
therefore I brought fire from your midst;
It devoured you, and I turned you to ashes upon the earth
In the sight of all who saw you."

Ezekiel 28:12–18 (NKJV)

Lucifer rose up against God and tried to set himself up as God. For his rebellion he was expelled from heaven. He became known as Satan (the adversary) or the devil. His punishment for rebelling against God, in addition to getting kicked out of heaven, will be spending eternity in the lake of fire.

> The devil, who deceived them, was cast into the lake of fire and brimstone where the beast and the false prophet are. And they will be tormented day and night forever and ever.
>
> Revelation 20:10 (NKJV)

According to myth, Satan is an ugly creature in a red suit with a pointy tail and horns who lives in hell. I'm not sure where that comes from, but I can assure you it is not true. He was actually a very beautiful creature when he was created. Remember we just called him the Angel of Light. I don't know what he looks like now, but I am sure that sin has changed him over the course of the thousands of years that have passed since his fall. It sounds as though he must be quite hideous.

> All who knew you among the peoples are astonished at you; You have become a horror, and shall be no more forever.
>
> Ezekiel 28:19 (NKJV)

He will not spend any time in hell or the lake of fire until he is actually forced to, though. The way he passes his time now is wandering around planet Earth looking for people to destroy.

> Be sober, be vigilant; because your adversary the devil walks about like a roaring lion, seeking whom he may devour.
>
> 1 Peter 5:8 (NKJV)

Notice that it says "like" a roaring lion. Contrary to what you may have seen in the movies or on TV, Satan is really not a very powerful being at all. He is not an equal but opposite force of God. He is a created being just like you and me. He has none of the attributes of God that we talked about in the second chapter. He is not omnipresent, omnipotent, infinite, or wise. He is not holy or righteous, and he is definitely not loving or good. As a matter of fact, his only real power is deception. He loves it when we portray him as some physically powerful being with amazing powers, but it is really all just part of his deception.

> Those who see you will gaze at you, and consider you, saying: "Is this the one who made the earth tremble, who shook the kingdoms?"
>
> Isaiah 14:16 (NKJV)

Remember he was the angel of light and he is such a deceiver that he has the natural ability to make evil and destructive things look real good, things that can destroy your life, but he whispers, "What can it hurt? Just this once. Who will ever know?"

One-third of the angels were kicked out of heaven with him. They are what we call demons or evil spirits. They all live in the spiritual world that is all around us; we just can't see it with our physical eyes. Satan and every one of his little partners hate all of mankind; they are very jealous of our position with God. Since they are headed for eternity in that lake of fire, they have determined to take as much of the human race with them as possible.

Satan and his forces cause all of the bad things that happen in this world. They can do it by whispering something in our ears, putting something enticing in front of our eyes, or putting us into a situation that will cause us to make bad choices and cause harm to ourselves or those around us. They also have had an indirect influence on our earth by the things that were set in motion at the fall of man and the influence of sin in the world, like disease, terrible weather, and earthquakes.

Since there are so many of these creatures, they are all around us all the time. They have watched you and studied you, and they know exactly what to put in front of you that will cause you to be tempted. That is the enticement we are talking about. Whatever it is you struggle with in life is what they will continue to harass you with. If you struggle with anger, they will make sure you are faced with events that cause you to get angry. If you struggle with sexual sins, they will make sure that you are surrounded by that temptation continually. Whatever is needed to make you stumble and fall and destroy your life, that is what they will do. And if they can get you to destroy someone else's life along the way, so much the better.

> The thief [Satan] does not come except to steal, and to kill, and to destroy.
>
> John 10:10a (NKJV)

Committing the Sin

The evil desire we have deep inside of us, combined with the enticement that Satan and his evil spirits bring, causes us to go ahead and follow through with the sinful act. Our evil desires and our evil actions are the result of our sin nature. All of those awesome qualities that God built into us are now defective and do not work as they were intended. So let's run down that list again, and this time we will look at what we have become because of sin.

The Consequences of Sin on Humans

God had a great plan and a great design, but because of sin we are now damaged goods. Everything God intended for good is now malfunctioning and is unable to perform at the peak efficiency of God's design.

God's Image in Man

Because of our fallen nature, God's image in us is now flawed.

Three in One

We still have a spirit, soul, and body, but now we have a fallen and sinful nature.

1. *Our Spirit.* This is the key element of our fallen nature. All of our other deficiencies originate in this one. God told Adam that when he ate from the tree in the middle of the garden he would surely die. It was in his spirit that this death took place. His spirit did not actually cease to exist—remember we are designed to live forever—but the relationship with God that he had been specifically designed for was now severed.

That is the state we all find ourselves in now. We were designed and created for a special relationship with God, and every one of us has been separated from God; the relationship we were designed for was cut off. Because of that broken relationship, we have a deep desire for spiritual things, but most of us have no idea that's what the problem is. If we are totally honest with ourselves though, we realize that we have an emptiness deep down inside of us that can never be filled and a sense of uneasiness and unfulfillment that is never satisfied.

That leaves us searching, looking for something to fill that empty spot. Even though there is nothing on this earth that can do it, we will strive continually to find it. We will try money, possessions, houses, cars, family, friends, sex, relationships, work, religion, pleasure, traveling, sports, achievements, drugs, drinking. You name it; we'll try it. But nothing works; it all leaves us empty. Notice that most of the things on this list are not in themselves bad; they just don't satisfy. Some of them are even important and necessary, but they still don't bring lasting fulfillment. For most of us, no matter how hard we work to make our life worthwhile, sooner or later we will end up disappointed.

There are lots of ways to hide our miserable and hopeless existence, though. We can stay busy, buy a few things, and have some fun. We can hang out with our friends and party as if there's no tomorrow. Drugs and alcohol will make us feel better, at least for a little while.

We live in a culture that honors hard work and rewards accomplishment, so most of us will do just that; we'll work hard, accomplish some things, and try to do something positive with our lives. We'll get married, have children, and find jobs. Some of us will be able to put together decent lives and might even attain a degree of happiness. But deep down inside, when no one is looking, there is still something missing. King Solomon put it this way:

> So what do people get for all their hard work? Their days of labor are filled with pain and grief; even at night they cannot rest. It is all utterly meaningless.
>
> Ecclesiastes 2:22–23 (NLT)

You can see the evidence of disappointment and failure all through our society. A very high percentage of our marriages end in divorce; drug and alcohol addictions are at epidemic levels; our families are filled with physical, emotional, and sexual abuse; and the suicide rate is as high or higher than it has been at any time in human history. And all of this is taking place in our Western society, where we are more blessed and prosperous than any culture ever.

2. *Our Soul.* Remember, this is where our thinking takes place and where our emotions and our willpower are located. It really is who we are. Our life is composed of a series of events and circumstances that determine how we live. Some of these are within our control, but many of them are not. It is not so much these events and circumstances in themselves that determine how we live; it is how we respond to them.

Our responder is in our soul. It is how we have learned to think and feel. It is what we know, what we believe, and how we make decisions. It is the way we act and the choices we make. We have developed habits that determine how we respond to certain stimuli. We are like a computer, and whatever is programmed inside of us determines what comes out. It determines if we get excited, if we get angry, if we are jealous, if we get upset, or if we are happy or sad.

In the third chapter we discussed how all of the

people in our lives have influenced who we are. One of the main ways they have influenced us is how we think. They have all had a huge influence on us, but what did we pick up from them? Have we learned to be optimistic people who have a positive outlook on life, or are we always negative, down on life, and down on people? Are we skeptical and cynical about everything, or are we hopeful and encouraging? Chances are, however, you think you're a product of the environment you grew up in. Unfortunately for most of us, what we learned was a lot of dreadful thinking.

A lot of us struggle with things like anger, depression, and feelings of inadequacy. All of those emotions are taking place in our soul.

3. *Our Body.* This one we each notice more and more as time goes by. When we start to get older, our bodies seem to deteriorate and fall apart right before our eyes. We get more aches and pains and maladies than we ever thought possible. The original bodies that God gave Adam and Eve were designed to last forever. Now our bodies are frail and vulnerable, and every one of us is going to die. We are plagued continually with sickness, injuries, diseases, deformities, and disabilities. Some of these are passed down from generation to generation, while others seem to just show up out of the blue or as the result of an accident. If we, or our family, or someone we know comes face to face with one of these ailments, we tend to blame God. The reality, though, is that he had nothing to do with it. It is not part of his plan or his design; it is the result of the fall of man and sin in the world.

A Desire for a Spiritual Connection with God

Because of the emptiness we feel deep inside from our severed relationship with God, we humans have a deep desire for spiritual things. Around the world, outside of Western culture, people are far more open to the possibility of a spiritual existence. When preachers and missionaries approach them with the gospel of Jesus Christ, they are far more likely to believe it and receive it. As a result there is huge growth around the world of people converting to Christianity and attending Christian churches. Here in the Western world, we tend to deny the spiritual, but things like the psychic hotline and the daily horoscope are enormously popular. We see huge growth in other religions, like Islam and Buddhism, while attendance in many Christian churches is on the decline.

People love TV shows, movies, and video games about the paranormal and unexplained phenomena. All of these show the fraudulent forms of the spiritual and the supernatural, but we would rather look to them to satisfy our spiritual hunger than turn to a God that might make some demands on how we live our lives.

Moral Character

As we have said before, we all have a moral conscience. God built in us the ability to know the difference between right and wrong. Even in our fallen state, I think most of us strive to do what is right most of the time. We don't always succeed, but the intentions are there. As we go through life, we are given more and more opportunities to see things and get involved in things that are not good for us. At first, when we make choices we know are not right, we feel really guilty. As we continue to make that choice, our conscience bothers us less and less, and soon we are able to do it without even a twinge of guilt. As our life goes by, we get involved with more and more things that we have learned to not let bother us, and eventually our conscience doesn't mess with us much at all. Here's how the Bible puts it: "Having their own conscience seared with a hot iron" (1 Timothy 4:2, NKJV).

When we begin making those bad choices and ignoring the warnings of our conscience, we are asking for trouble. Bad behavior becomes part of our lifestyle, and we are traveling down a road that leads to destruction. It will take us to places we never wanted to go, it will have us doing things we never thought we would do, and it will keep us there longer than we ever wanted to stay. As a matter of fact, in most cases it won't let us go at all, no matter how hard we try to get free.

The Ability to Reason

We live in a day and age when knowledge is increasing at such an incredible speed we can't keep up with it. Our computers and other high-tech gadgets are outdated almost the minute we buy them. This laptop I am using has more capability than the computer that filled an entire room when I went to college. We know more about how things work now than anyone in history has ever even dreamed of.

This is what we have put our faith in; this is what we trust. We believe in science and technology. We love to collect information. We take our information and develop knowledge. Then we formulate what we consider to be truth, based on our knowledge. Most of us don't have a lot of actual scientific expertise, so we base our understanding of truth and knowledge on the opinions of others. I guess we just hope or naïvely believe that our expert doesn't have a hidden agenda. The problem is we can find an expert to back up whatever point of view we want to take.

We don't leave much room in our thinking for the supernatural, the faith based, or the spiritual. Here is how many people in the world today have learned to think: *There might have been some unexplained events in our world and in our history that we would consider a curiosity or a novelty, but they could be reasonably understood and explained if we had all the facts. In my thinking, if it is verifiable by science, then it must be true, and conversely if it cannot be verified, then it must not be true. It's okay for others to believe in that religious hocus pocus, but if people had any sense at all, they would realize that it is all a bunch of nonsense. Any logical person knows that there is no God and that the Bible is a bunch of archaic stories and myths. The ancient people were just trying to explain things they weren't able to understand at that time.*

And don't even try to give me a list of rules based on some ridiculous ancient writings. You can't lay out a bunch of requirements for how to live and say they apply to everyone. They aren't relevant in today's world anyway; we're a lot more intelligent than that now. We have come to the realization that there are no definite rights and wrongs. Things are a lot more subjective than that, and it is up to each of us to make our own decisions on our morality. We are all different, and we all have our own beliefs.

Our Instincts

Because of our sinful natures, the instincts that God placed within us for our survival are now perverted. What God gave us to make our continued existence on earth possible are now the root of our thoughtless and selfish lives. Let's look at what our built-in instincts have become.

Self-preservation. We have a drive to stay alive. In our fallen nature, it manifests itself in our self-centeredness. Our society tells us, "Look out for number one" and, "If you don't look out for yourself, no one else will." We are totally and completely selfish and self-centered. We are looking for ways to make ourselves happy, so we will do whatever it takes to bring ourselves pleasure. For some of us, hard work brings us pleasure, and we will sacrifice everything else for the job. For others of us it might be money or possessions, so we spend all of our energies trying to collect more. Some of us might put our family or our homes at the center of everything, but it all better be functioning the way we think it should, or we're going to be disappointed, angry, and depressed. We might think entertainment will make us happy, so we'll turn to sports, music, TV, the movies, and video games. Some of us love to go out on the town and party till the sun comes up. Some of us want to travel the world looking for adventure and excitement.

For all of us, a tee shirt that reads, "Yes, as a matter of fact the world does revolve around me!" would be perfect. We like to have what we want, when we want it, how we want it. Our normal response when our expectations are not met and we are not getting our way is anger. Actually anger is part of God's image built inside of us. The Bible tells us that God does get angry. However, God's anger is always justified. He gets angry over immorality and injustice. Our anger, on the other hand, is normally unjustified because it is wrapped up in our own selfishness. Someone or something didn't act the way we wanted them to, and now we're mad.

Gathering. We love to acquire stuff. Not just for survival, but just to have stuff. We have more belongings than any person really needs, and still we want more. Our culture is totally consumed with materialism. Amazingly, we judge ourselves and others on our ability to accumulate things. Somehow in our thinking, collecting stuff means success. In our attempts to fill that empty spot we were talking about earlier, we try to use possessions. We think that a new car, a new truck, a new boat, a new house, new furniture, a new jet ski, a new golf club, a new rifle, a new dress, a new sweater, a new pair of shoes, or a new pair of jeans is somehow going to make us happy. Unfortunately, with any of these items the happiness is short lived. It isn't long before the newness wears off, and we are looking for something else to make us happy and fill the void.

There are a couple of other emotions here that might rear their ugly heads as well. They are jealousy and envy. Jealousy is the unreasonable worry that someone is going to come and take the stuff away from us that we have already collected. Envy is seeing the stuff that someone else has collected and wanting it for ourselves. In some cases we might even resort to stealing it if we can't find a way to acquire it by legitimate means.

Food and Water. We live in an overindulgent society, and we love to eat and drink. We need food and water to survive, but we have taken it to all-new levels. As a culture, we throw away more than anyone else in the world consumes. We are overweight and out of shape. Our restaurants and bars are packed most of the time, and food and drink are at the center of almost all of our activities. Sometimes I think the emptiness we feel inside of ourselves is hunger or thirst. Unfortunately, there is nothing that we can eat or drink that will fill that void. But we'll keep trying.

Reproduction. We talked about God's wonderful design of the sexual relationship between a man and a woman in the context of marriage. However, since the sex drive God placed within us is such a huge part of our life, in our fallen nature things can get out of whack pretty quickly.

It's not that sex in itself is bad. Sex is God's idea and God's design, but it has to be used according to his plan. Anything outside of that is distorted and destructive. Unfortunately, that is all we see in the public arena. The temptation to get involved in something that will destroy God's design for our lives is in our faces almost constantly. God wants us to have a good life, and Satan wants to destroy it. Guess where the enticement to get involved with something that will mess us up comes from? It is one of his greatest weapons, and Satan attacks us with it repeatedly. Sex has become such an intrinsic part of our culture that we are under constant bombardment. Since our sexual urges are part of who we are, we are usually pretty easy prey.

In our modern culture, sexual relationships outside of marriage are accepted behavior; they are thought to be normal and expected. If anything is said that disagrees, it is ridiculed as being old fashioned and out of touch with reality. God's plan for sex within marriage is good. Unfortunately, we haven't listened, and we see the results in our society of doing things our own way. Divorce rates are higher than they have ever been, and they continue to rise. Unplanned pregnancies, abortions, and sexually transmitted diseases continue in epidemic proportions. Sexual abuse and sexual assaults occur with such growing regularity that we are at a loss what to do about it.

Dominance. God placed within us the drive to be in control of our lives and our environments so we could survive on planet Earth. He gave us control over our planet so we could use it for our survival. Now, in our fallen nature, our ability to control turns to selfishness, abuse, anger, tyranny, injustice, and murder. We're driven by the lust for money and power. If anything stands in the way of us getting what we want, when we want it, we will run over it. Over the course of our history, we have shown the ability to destroy people, destroy our environment, destroy cultures, and destroy civilizations. We look at the people who have done these things and judge them as being horrible, out-of-control people, but if we do not learn to control our own lives, we have the ability to destroy our marriages, destroy our families, and destroy ourselves.

Our Temperaments

In each of our built-in, God-given temperaments we talked about in the last chapter, there are strengths and weaknesses. Unfortunately, in the fallen state we all find ourselves living in now, our weaknesses seem to control who we are. Let's look at each of the temperaments to see what dominates our lives now.

Melancholy. Because Melancholies are very perfectionistic, they are also very demanding and critical. They have very high expectations of how things need to be arranged and taken care of, and anything other than the ideal is met with anger and ridicule. Their ideals are so high that they can't even live up to them themselves, so they tend to suffer from a low self-esteem. They are thinkers, so they can take a negative thought and dwell on it until they drive themselves into a deep depression. It is common for them to have substance-abuse problems because they are looking for something to help them cope with a complex and difficult life. They prefer to be alone rather than in crowds of people, so they tend to be loners. Their natural creativity will probably have a negative quality to it because it reflects their own tendency to look at life from the dark and pessimistic side.

Choleric. These leaders are sure that they have the greatest ideas and are certain that they know the best way of getting things done. Because they are so self-assured, they tend to be impatient, stubborn, and overbearing. They are demanding and insensitive and tend to be people abusers. They are workaholics who stay away from close relationships and avoid seeking help from others. They need to be in control in whatever situation they find themselves in and are unwilling to submit to the authority of another.

Sanguine. These party animals will put being where the action is ahead of responsibilities. If the opportunity to socialize arises, they will drop whatever they are doing and head for the party. If that happens to be work, school, chores, or family, oh well. If they have to let a few bills slide to get a new pair of shoes or a new outfit, that is fine too. If they have made an arrangement to meet you for lunch and something else comes up, they'll forget all about you. They didn't mean to hurt your feelings; they just got a better offer. They are shallow, phony, and prone to exaggeration. They are selfish, easily bored, and if they need something from you, are very good manipulators. It is common for them to have substance-abuse problems too, because for them it is a way of fitting in.

Phlegmatic. These easygoing people are also very stubborn. They like life to be easy and uncomplicated and if someone is making demands of them and pushes them to go places or do things they don't want to, they will just dig their heals in and refuse. Because they like life to be trouble-free and undemanding, they have a tendency to be observers of life rather than participants. They tend to be lazy and unsupportive and willing to watch others work, rather than step in and lend a hand. They are also indecisive and guarded.

Men and Women

God's plan and design was for the differences between men and women to fit together and fulfill a common purpose. In our fallen and sinful natures, our differences become sources of conflict, jealously, anger, and abuse. We fight over our roles, positions, and responsibilities. We take the positions God gave us in our families and use them against each other. God gave men the position of provider and protector for his family, and men turn that into abuse and control. He gave women the role of nourisher and comforter for her family, which turns that into impatience and resentment.

Men take their capability to compartmentalize their lives into the ability to get involved in things they shouldn't. They can put pornography and sexual immorality into one of their boxes and think it has nothing to do with the rest of their lives. They can have drug and alcohol boxes, anger boxes, and mean boxes. Because they are looking for easy boxes, they can be neglectful and lazy when it comes to living up to their responsibilities. Men can still feel good about themselves if they are able to bring about some level of success in their efforts to accomplish something with their lives, even if things are not going that well at home. On the other hand, if they are unsuccessful out in the working world, they could suffer from feelings of disillusionment, incompetence, and frustration.

Because women are relationship oriented, they are always trying to change their husband and help him be a better man, husband, father, worker, etc. They think that if they criticize or nag loud enough and long enough, their husbands will eventually change their ways. Women will try to change their children the same way but will add discipline and punishment to their methods. They can use crying, yelling, screaming, coldness, and withdrawal from the relationship in hopes that the family will conform to their wishes. When they find that the husband and children are not measuring up, they tend to become more and more critical. They will dwell on the negatives instead of appreciating the good things about their family members. A woman could be the CEO of a major corporation, but if things are not going well at home, she will have feelings of disappointment, inadequacy, and depression.

Probably the worst abuse of God's design for men and women is when they give up trying to blend their differences and become attracted to the same sex instead. I am sure that there are many contributing factors to why a person would get caught up in that lifestyle; but it is a counterfeit version of God's original plan, and it only leads to frustration and destruction. Just like all of the other wrong choices we make in life, it is based on our fallen nature and the deception of our enemy, Satan.

> So God let them go ahead and do whatever shameful things their hearts desired. As a result, they did vile and degrading things with each other's bodies. Instead of believing what they knew was the truth about God, they deliberately chose to believe lies. That is why God abandoned them to their shameful desires. Even the women turned against the natural way to have sex and instead indulged in sex with each other. And the men, instead of having normal sexual relationships with women, burned with lust for each other. Men did shameful things with other men and, as a result, suffered within themselves the penalty they so richly deserved.
>
> Romans 1:24–27 (NLT)

The only true and satisfying relationship available in this world is for a man and a woman to work through those differences that God created in them and to use those differences to strengthen their relationship with each other. This requires a lot of patience and perseverance because it could take years. There are no shortcuts to a happy relationship. Anytime you quit one relationship and begin another, you go back to square one and start the process all over again. The only way to true happiness is to stay with a relationship long enough to make it work.

Eternal Consequences of Sin

It has been established in the Word of God that, when our time on earth is over, we will all stand in front of God and answer for our lives. The Bible calls this place the Great White Throne. It is going to be a terrifying place where we will have to answer for the lives we lead during our lifetimes on earth.

> And I saw a Great White Throne, and I saw the one who was sitting on it. The earth and sky fled from his presence, but they found no place to hide. I saw the dead, both great and small, standing before God's Throne. And the books were opened, including the Book of Life. And the dead were judged according to the things written in the books, according to what they had done. The sea gave up the dead in it, and death and the grave gave up the dead in them. They were all judged according to their deeds. And death and the grave were thrown into the lake of fire. This is the second death—the lake of fire. And anyone whose name was not found recorded in the Book of Life was thrown into the lake of fire.
>
> Revelation 20:11–15 (NLT)

God has books where the events of our lives are recorded and another book called the Book of Life, where the names of those who have accepted Jesus are listed. We get to stand trial in front of the God of the universe himself. Doesn't that sound exciting? We will be asked the question "What did you do with my Son, Jesus?" God already knows the answer to that question, but he is going to ask you anyway. It is kind of like when you are standing in front of a judge here on earth and are asked, "How do you plead?" After you answer his question, you will be given an opportunity to state your case. When you are finished, he will open the books and show you all of the evidence he has against you, all of the times you were given the opportunity to believe God and put your trust in him. After the trial of your life is over, he will check the Book of Life to see if your name is in it. If not, you will be declared guilty of all the charges against you, and you will be sentenced to the place of eternal punishment, the lake of fire.

As long as earth continues to exist in the way we are living now, those who have died without a relationship with Jesus are in a place called hell. When our current way of living has run its course and we move into the next age, the Bible says that death, hell, and the grave will be thrown into the lake of fire.

Here are some of the ways the Bible describes this eternal judgment: the second death, a place of suffering and pain, weeping and gnashing of teeth, hopelessness, and loneliness. It all sounds very unpleasant, doesn't it? The thing is, none of it was intended for mankind. It was designed for Satan and all of his fallen angels. Satan is determined to take as many of God's special creation with him as he can, and we let him get away with it. God made a way of escape for us, and if you haven't accepted it yet, allow yourself to be open to receive as we go through God's plan of redemption for us in chapter five.

Conclusion

It sounds as though there is not much hope in this life, doesn't it? I purposely made this chapter as gloomy and depressing as I could. As I have mentioned, most of us in our Western culture consider ourselves to be pretty self-reliant. We think we can figure out life on our own, and we don't need much help from others. We definitely don't think some old-fashioned religion is the answer; that is just a crutch for the weak who are not able make it on their own. What we all need to realize is what an utterly hopeless state we are actually in.

As we were going through the consequences of our fallen nature, I'm sure most of you were thinking, *I'm not as bad as that, at least most of the time!* That's the deal. We aren't that bad all of the time, but we are sometimes. We were created in the image of God, and we have many good things in our lives because of it. But we also have a fallen and sinful nature and have many not-so-good things in our lives as well. As a matter of fact, we don't even really know how good or how bad we actually are. Until we face certain situations, we'll never really know how good we can be or how truly evil we can be. We have both of them deep inside of us.

As we go through our daily lives, most of us try to do things right. We want to do well, and we want to succeed. We want to do good, and we do not want to do evil. Unfortunately, as most of us have probably noticed, we are not very successful at it. We have the best intentions, but not much follow-through. Our good intentions are because of God's image in us. Our lack of follow-through and our bad behavior are the result of our sinful nature. Here is how Paul put it in the book of Romans:

> I don't understand myself at all, for I really want to do what is right, but I don't do it. Instead, I do the very thing I hate. I know perfectly well that what I am doing is wrong, and my bad conscience shows that I agree that the law is good. But I can't help myself, because it is sin inside me that makes me do these evil things.
>
> I know I am rotten through and through so far as my old sinful nature is concerned. No matter which way I turn, I can't make myself do right. I want to, but I can't. When I want to do good, I don't. And when I try not to do wrong, I do it anyway. But if I am doing what I don't want to do, I am not really the one doing it; the sin within me is doing it. It seems to be a fact of life that when I want to do what is right, I inevitably do what is wrong.
>
> I love God's law with all my heart. But there is another law at work within me that is at war with my mind. This law wins the fight and makes me a slave to the sin that is still within me. Oh, what a miserable person I am! Who will free me from this life that is dominated by sin?
>
> Romans 7:15–24 (NLT)

So, who is going to free us? Are we destined to a life of struggle and despair? Should we just turn to a life of drugs and alcohol to mask our misery? Paul has the answer for us in the very next verse. "Thank God! The answer is in Jesus Christ our Lord" (Romans 7:25, NLT). Let's move on now and find out what God did to rescue us from this terrible dilemma we find ourselves in.

God's Plan for Our Salvation

> For God so loved the world that He gave His only begotten Son, that whoever believes in Him should not perish but have everlasting life.
>
> John 3:16 (NKJV)

Principle 5 – As Christians we believe that Jesus, the Messiah, is God come in the flesh. His purpose for coming was to bring us back into a right relationship with God and defeat the power of sin in our lives.

I once heard the story of a farmer who was looking out of his farm-house window watching a storm that was passing through his area. He noticed there was a funnel cloud circling right in front of his barn, and as he was studying the cloud with great interest, he realized there was a group of small birds caught in the funnel with no way of escape. He saw how helpless they were in the storm, and he observed that the window to the loft of his barn was right near where the birds were caught in the storm. *If those birds could make their way to the window of the loft, they would be safe,* he thought.

As he continued to watch them, he realized they

did not see or understand how to escape the storm and get to safety. He was feeling very sorry for the birds and then suddenly he had another idea. *If only I could become one of them*, he thought. *Then I could fly in there, lead them out of the storm, and get them to safety!*

As he was considering this, he realized that is exactly what God did for us. He saw the predicament we are in, and he became one of us so he could rescue us from this life of hopelessness and confusion we find ourselves in and lead us to safety.

> But when He saw the multitudes, He was moved with compassion for them, because they were weary and scattered, like sheep having no shepherd.
>
> Matthew 9:36 (NKJV)

> Then Jesus said, "Come to me, all of you who are weary and carry heavy burdens, and I will give you rest."
>
> Matthew 11:28 (NLT)

God looked out of the windows of heaven and saw us and the pitiful condition we are all in. He had compassion on us and took human form to rescue us from our life of hopelessness. This is how God chose to bring us back into the relationship we were designed for. We were designed to have a special connection with God, and, as we have learned, sin destroyed that. On our own, we have no way to restore that relationship. We are lost, hopeless, broken, and empty. So God stepped in:

> But God, who is rich in mercy, because of His great love with which He loved us, even when we were dead in trespasses, made us alive together with Christ (by grace you have been saved).
>
> Ephesians 2:4–5 (NKJV)

> But God demonstrates His own love toward us, in that while we were still sinners, Christ died for us.
>
> Romans 5:8 (NKJV)

He didn't wait for us to get our act together. He knew there was no way for us to get our act together. He came to our rescue and sent the answer to us. That answer is Jesus. He is the answer to all of our struggles and all of our problems. All of the difficulties of this life can be dealt with when we turn our lives over to Jesus and learn to conform to his design for our lives. In this chapter we will learn about Jesus, who he is, why he came, and what he will do for us if we choose to believe him.

His Names

Just like chapter two, when we learned about the names of God, the names of Jesus used in the Bible describe who he is.

Jesus

Jeshua (Yeshua) in Hebrew. This is his name, and it means *salvation.* The name itself portrayed to the

Jews that Jesus had come to be a savior to the Jewish people.

> And she will bring forth a Son, and you shall call His name Jesus, for He will save His people from their sins.
>
> Matthew 1:21 (NKJV)

This is the name he went by while he was living here on earth. You might have heard him referred to as Jesus of Nazareth. That is his name combined with the town he grew up in; Nazareth, in the region of Israel known as Galilee.

The Christ

Christos in Greek. Some people think that Christ is Jesus's last name; many have only heard it used as a curse word. *Christos* is the Greek translation of the Hebrew word *Messiah.* It means "The Anointed One." It is how we got our name Christian, or followers of Christos.

> It was there at Antioch that the believers were first called Christians.
>
> Acts 11:26 (NLT)

The Jewish nation has been waiting for centuries for its Messiah. The anointed one from God who will come and rescue them from servanthood to other nations, set himself up as their king, and establish Israel as a mighty nation in the world. This has been prophesied from the very beginnings of the human race and is deeply rooted in Israel's culture. There are many prophecies about the coming of the Messiah throughout the Old Testament. The very first one was way back in the Garden of Eden.

God was talking to Satan in the form of the serpent when he said: "From now on, you and the woman will be enemies, and your offspring and her offspring will be enemies. He will crush your head, and you will strike his heel." Genesis 3:15 (NLT)

God had given mankind dominion over the earth, and man had relinquished that to Satan in the garden. God was telling Satan that one of the descendants of the woman, Jesus, was going to crush his head. Crushing Satan's head represented taking away the authority he had taken from mankind. Striking his heal was talking about Satan's attempt to do away with Jesus at the crucifixion.

Many of the prophecies tell about the Messiah coming to be a great ruler and king. The people of Israel really love these prophecies and are anxiously awaiting their fulfillment. These were all written several hundred years before the time of Jesus.

> For unto us a Child is born, unto us a Son is given; and the government will be upon his shoulder. And His name will be called Wonderful, Counselor, Mighty God, Everlasting Father, Prince of Peace. Of the increase of His government and peace there will be no end, upon the throne of David and over His kingdom, to order it and establish it with judgment and justice from that time forward, even forever.
>
> Isaiah 9:6–7 (NKJV)

> There shall come forth a Rod from the stem of Jesse, and a Branch shall grow out of his roots. The Spirit of the LORD shall rest upon Him, the Spirit of wisdom and understanding, the Spirit of counsel and might, the Spirit of knowledge and of the fear of the LORD. His delight is in the fear of the LORD, and He shall not judge by the sight of His eyes, nor decide by the hearing of His ears; but with righteousness he shall judge the poor, and decide with equity for the meek of the earth; he shall strike the earth with the rod of His mouth, and with the breath of His lips He shall slay the wicked. Righteousness shall be the belt of His loins, and faithfulness the belt of His waist.
>
> Isaiah 11:1–5 (NKJV)

> "Behold, the days are coming," says the LORD, "That I will raise to David a Branch of righteousness; a King shall reign and prosper, and execute judgment and righteousness in the earth. In His days Judah will be saved, and Israel will dwell safely; now this is His name by which He will be called: THE LORD OUR RIGHTEOUSNESS."
>
> Jeremiah 23:5–6 (NKJV)

These are just a few of the many prophesies of the coming of the Jewish messiah. They are still waiting for him. The Bible says that one day the nation of Israel will realize that they were deceived and that Jesus truly is their messiah. It says that they will all believe him and turn to him on the very same day. What a great day that will be. I wonder if it would have a lot more meaning if our English translations would have called him "Jesus the Messiah" rather than "Jesus Christ."

The Son of God

One born of God. This separates Jesus from all of the other prophets and religious leaders in the history of the world. The existence of Jesus is proven by history. There are accounts of him in other ancient Roman documents besides the Bible, so we know the man is an actual historical figure. There are many who will admit that Jesus was a prophet and a great teacher with revolutionary concepts about God and our relationship to God. But they really miss the point. Jesus claimed to be the Son of God! What would that make him if he weren't? How can a man be considered a prophet and a great teacher if he walks around claiming to be the Son of God? He would have to be crazy. It would make him just one more of the thousands of religious nut jobs we've seen down through history. You don't believe any of the silly people you see standing on the side of the road calling themselves the messiah, do you? So why should we believe this Jesus?

The Bible says that Jesus was the Son of God. God said it about him, Jesus said it about himself, and his followers called him the Son of God.

1. *The Angel Called Jesus the Son of God.* The angel Gabriel appeared to Mary and told her she was going to have a child and that he would be the Son of God.

   And the angel answered and said to her, "The Holy Spirit will come upon you, and the power of the Highest will overshadow you; therefore, also, that Holy One who is to be born will be called the Son of God."

Luke 1:35 (NKJV)

2. *God Calls Jesus His Son.*

And suddenly a voice came from heaven, saying, "This is My beloved Son, in whom I am well pleased."

Matthew 3:17 (NKJV)

3. *Jesus Calls Himself God's Son.*

When Jesus had finished saying all these things, he looked up to heaven and said, "Father, the time has come. Glorify your Son so he can give glory back to you. For you have given him authority over everyone in all the earth. He gives eternal life to each one you have given him. And this is the way to have eternal life—to know you, the only true God, and Jesus Christ, the one you sent to earth. I brought glory to you here on earth by doing everything you told me to do. And now, Father, bring me into the glory we shared before the world began."

John 17:1–5 (NLT)

4. *His Followers Claimed He Was the Son of God.*

Simon Peter answered and said, "You are the Christ, the Son of the living God."

Matthew 16:16 (NKJV)

She said to Him, "Yes, Lord, I believe that You are the Christ, the Son of God, who is to come into the world."

John 11:27 (NKJV)

The Son of Man

When Jesus referred to himself as the Son of Man, he was saying, "I am the Son of God come in the flesh, with a human nature and human qualities."

> But Jesus, knowing their thoughts, said, "Why do you think evil in your hearts? For which is easier, to say, 'Your sins are forgiven you,' or to say, 'Arise and walk'? But that you may know that the Son of Man has power on earth to forgive sins"—then He said to the paralytic, "Arise, take up your bed, and go to your house." And he arose and departed to his house.
>
> Matthew 9:4–7 (NKJV)

There are two very important principles of the Christian faith that are established by the humanity of Jesus, and they are both based on his virgin birth. Some dismiss the virgin birth as a fairytale or a myth, but without it none of what Jesus accomplished by coming to earth would be possible.

The first is this: the Bible says that our sinful nature was passed down through our fathers.

> For I, the LORD your God, am a jealous God, visiting the iniquity of the fathers upon the children to the third and fourth generations of those who hate Me.
>
> Exodus 20:5 (NKJV)

> Our fathers sinned and are no more, but we bear their iniquities.
>
> Lamentations 5:7 (NKJV)

> Prepare slaughter for his children because of the iniquity of their fathers.
>
> Isaiah 14:21 (NKJV)

> The fathers have eaten sour grapes, and the children's teeth are set on edge.
>
> Ezekiel 18:2 (NKJV)

The sinful nature we all inherited from Adam and Eve is passed down through our fathers, and we fathers are passing them down to our children. Since Jesus didn't have an earthly father, the sinful nature was not passed down to him, so he was born without sin.

Second, since he had a human mother, he was born as a human being. He was born with a completely human body with all of its limitations and frailties. In chapter three we described how God originally created mankind before sin entered the world and changed us. That is how Jesus was; since he was born without sin, he had all of the attributes of man without the influence of sin.

> Let this mind be in you which was also in Christ Jesus, who, being in the form of God, did not consider it robbery to be equal with God, but made Himself of no reputation, taking the form of a bondservant, and coming in the likeness of men. And being found in appearance as a man, He humbled Himself and became obedient to the point of death, even the death of the cross.
>
> Philippians 2:5–8 (NKJV)

Jesus set aside his deity, his godly powers, to become a man. During the time he lived here on earth, he chose to live as a human being and did not use his abilities as God. He had to live with the frailties and weaknesses of the human body just as we do. And he had to live with the same temptations to get off track and mess up our lives. The only difference is he succeeded at it. We never do.

He did perform many miracles while he was here, but he did them in the same way we can do them, through the power of the Holy Spirit. We'll talk more about that in the next chapter.

The Son of David

This indicates Jesus' human ancestry. David was the greatest king in Israel's history. You've probably heard of David and Goliath. That is only one of the stories of his life recorded in the books of 1 and 2 Samuel, 1 Kings, and 1 Chronicles. He was called, "A man after God's own heart." Because of David's faithfulness, he was promised that he would always have a son sitting on the throne of Israel. For a while his sons and descendents were kings, but the true fulfillment of the promise is Jesus the Messiah. The book of Matthew records the ancestry of his earthly stepfather, Joseph, and Luke records the ancestry of his mother, Mary. Both are descended from David. He is directly descended from King David, and he will rule forever.

The Word

In the first chapter of the book of John, there is an interesting and somewhat confusing set of verses that talk about the Word of God becoming flesh and dwelling among us.

> In the beginning was the Word, and the Word was with God, and the Word was God. He was in the beginning with God. All things were made through Him, and without Him nothing was made that was made. In Him was life, and the life was the light of men. And the light shines in the darkness, and the darkness did not comprehend it... And the Word became flesh and dwelt among us, and we beheld His glory, the glory as of the only begotten of the Father, full of grace and truth.
>
> John 1:1–5, 14 (NKJV)

The "Word" is referring to Jesus. We can see from these verses that he was at the very beginning with God, and as a matter of fact, he is God. And we can also see that everything in the world was made by him. Maybe we could read it this way:

> In the beginning was *Jesus,* and *Jesus* was with God, and *Jesus* was God. He was in the beginning with God. All things were made through Him, and without Him nothing was made that was made. In Him was life, and the life was the light of men. And the light shines in the darkness, and the darkness did not comprehend it... And *Jesus* became flesh and dwelt among us, and we beheld His glory, the glory as of the only begotten of the Father, full of grace and truth.
>
> John 1:1–5, 14 (NKJV, emphasis added)

We can also look at it this way: the spoken and written word is how we express ourselves. It is how we communicate with others, how we tell them what we are thinking, how we feel, and what we want. So Jesus is the Word of God.

This is how God expresses himself and how he communicates with us about how he feels, what he is thinking, and what he wants. If you want to know about God, learn about Jesus.

Kurios

This is the Greek word for *Lord.* It means deity or God, someone having the divine nature and power of God. In the Roman Empire, they used this word when they referred to Caesar. They considered him to be God, and they called him Lord Caesar. It caused them a little concern to hear *Kurios* used in reference to Jesus.

Okay, so God sent his Son to Earth. He set aside his godly powers and abilities to live here as man. He is the Messiah that the Jews have been waiting for, the Savior of the world, and the Word of God come in the flesh. But what does all that have to do with me? Even if I believe it is all true, how does it affect my life? Let's look at that now. What did his coming accomplish?

The Accomplishments and Purposes of Jesus

Jesus came to earth and lived as a man. Through his life he showed and taught us how to live our lives. Through his death he defeated sin, sickness, unhealthy living, and destructive behavior in each of our lives. Through his resurrection he defeated the power of Satan in our lives. Through his ascension into heaven, he gave us the power to live a victorious Christian life every day. Let's look at each one of these up close.

His Life

God came to earth and showed us how to live and survive on earth. The first man, Adam, struggled and failed. Ever since that time we have all been struggling and failing. We need to be taught how to live, how to act, how to treat each other, how to prioritize our lives, and how to live successfully.

The Bible calls him a rabbi or teacher, and it calls his followers disciples. The Greek word that is translated *disciple* means "followers of a teacher that not only listen to his words, but follow his example and learn to live just like he does." Jesus spent his time loving people, serving people, and caring for people. He taught them how to live, he healed their diseases, and he prayed for their lives. He showed by his example how we are to center our lives around God and how to put serving others ahead of serving ourselves.

There was a popular little slogan a few years ago called WWJD (What Would Jesus Do?). It came to be ridiculed after a while, and people have taken it to extremes, like "What would Jesus Drive," but it is actually a command in the Bible.

> I have given you an example to follow. Do as I have done to you.
>
> John 13:15 (NLT)

> Imitate me [Paul], just as I also imitate Christ.
>
> 1 Corinthians 11:1 (NKJV)

He even told us that we would be able to do the same kind of miracles he did.

> The truth is, anyone who believes in me will do the same works I have done, and even greater works, because I am going to be with the Father.
>
> John 14:12 (NLT)

If we could learn to pattern our lives after the life of Jesus, we would find that our lives and our relationships with others would go a whole lot better.

His Death

The Bible says that this is the reason Jesus came and it began the process of restoring us into a right relationship with God.

It was established from the very beginning that blood has to be shed for sin to be forgiven and someone has to die as punishment for sin. That may seem rather harsh and hard to understand, but it has been ordained by God as the only just way of dealing with sin.

> Without the shedding of blood, there is no forgiveness of sins.
>
> Hebrews 9:22 (NLT)

> For the wages of sin is death, but the gift of God is eternal life in Christ Jesus our Lord.
>
> Romans 6:23 (NKJV)

In the Old Testament, God made an arrangement with the Israelites to use the shed blood of an animal to have their sins forgiven. When they followed God's plan, their sins were forgiven and covered for one year.

> The LORD said to Moses, "Warn your brother Aaron not to enter the Most Holy Place behind the inner curtain whenever he chooses; the penalty for intrusion is death. For the Ark's cover—the place of atonement—is there, and I myself am present in the cloud over the atonement cover.
>
> "When Aaron enters the sanctuary area, he must follow these instructions fully. He must first bring a young bull for a sin offering and a ram for a whole burnt offering ... The people of Israel must then bring him two male goats for a sin offering and a ram for a whole burnt offering.
>
> "Aaron will present the bull as a sin offering, to make atonement for himself and his family. Then he must bring the two male goats and present them to the Lord at the entrance of the Tabernacle. He is to cast sacred lots to determine which goat will be sacrificed to the LORD and which one will be the scapegoat. The goat chosen to be sacrificed to the LORD will be presented by Aaron as a sin offering. The goat chosen to be the scapegoat will be presented to the LORD alive. When it is sent away into the wilderness, it will make atonement for the people.
>
> "Then Aaron will present the young bull as a sin offering for himself and his family. After he has slaughtered this bull for the sin offering, he will fill an incense burner with burning coals from the altar that stands before the LORD. Then, after fill-

ing both his hands with fragrant incense, he will carry the burner and incense behind the inner curtain. There in the LORD's presence, he will put the incense on the burning coals so that a cloud of incense will rise over the Ark's cover—the place of atonement—that rests on the Ark of the Covenant. If he follows these instructions, he will not die. Then he must dip his finger into the blood of the bull and sprinkle it on the front of the atonement cover and then seven times against the front of the Ark.

"Then Aaron must slaughter the goat as a sin offering for the people and bring its blood behind the inner curtain. There he will sprinkle the blood on the atonement cover and against the front of the Ark, just as he did with the bull's blood. In this way, he will make atonement for the Most Holy Place, and he will do the same for the entire Tabernacle, because of the defiling sin and rebellion of the Israelites. No one else is allowed inside the Tabernacle while Aaron goes in to make atonement for the Most Holy Place. No one may enter until he comes out again after making atonement for himself, his family, and all the Israelites.

"Then Aaron will go out to make atonement for the altar that stands before the LORD by smearing some of the blood from the bull and the goat on each of the altar's horns. Then he must dip his finger into the blood and sprinkle it seven times over the altar. In this way, he will cleanse it from Israel's defilement and return it to its former holiness …

"The bull and goat given as sin offerings, whose blood Aaron brought into the Most Holy Place to

> make atonement for Israel, will be carried outside the camp to be burned. This includes the animals' hides, the internal organs, and the dung. The man who does the burning must wash his clothes and bathe himself in water before returning to the camp …
>
> This is a permanent law for you, to make atonement for the Israelites once each year."
>
> Leviticus 16:2–3, 5–19, 27–28, 34 (NLT)

The Israelite nation had to go through this long, difficult, and imperfect process that had to be repeated once each year.

Then in the New Testament, God gave us a new plan. A better word for *testament* is *covenant.* So the New Covenant is God's new promise to all of us to forgive our sins and bring us back into a permanent relationship with him. He sent Jesus into the world to be the sacrifice for all of our sins.

> For God so loved the world that He gave His only begotten Son, that whoever believes in Him should not perish but have everlasting life.
>
> John 3:16 (NKJV)

Jesus came to earth, was born without sin, and lived a perfect, sin-free life. Then he took all of our sins upon himself and died on the cross in our place. After he died, he went into heaven, and acting as the high Priest, the same as Aaron was for the people of Israel, Jesus went into the most holy place. There, instead of the blood of goats and bulls, he took his own blood and made atonement for all of our sins.

This time it was permanent. The earthly process had to be repeated each year; Jesus did it in heaven one time for all of us. It never has to be done again.

> So Christ has now become the High Priest over all the good things that have come. He has entered that great, perfect sanctuary in heaven, not made by human hands and not part of this created world. Once for all time he took blood into that Most Holy Place, but not the blood of goats and calves. He took his own blood, and with it he secured our salvation forever.
>
> Under the old system, the blood of goats and bulls and the ashes of a young cow could cleanse people's bodies from ritual defilement. Just think how much more the blood of Christ will purify our hearts from deeds that lead to death so that we can worship the living God. For by the power of the eternal Spirit, Christ offered himself to God as a perfect sacrifice for our sins. That is why he is the one who mediates the new covenant between God and people, so that all who are invited can receive the eternal inheritance God has promised them. For Christ died to set them free from the penalty of the sins they had committed under that first covenant.
>
> Hebrews 9:11–15 (NLT)

Jesus died in our place. We do not have to face the consequence of our sin because he did it for us. About seven hundred years before Jesus even came to earth, the prophet Isaiah wrote about his crucifixion. It is amazing how exact his prophecy is to what we read about the actual event in the New Testament accounts. Isaiah explains what Jesus accomplished for us by what he went through.

> He is despised and rejected by men, a Man of sorrows and acquainted with grief. And we hid, as it were, our faces from Him; he was despised, and we did not esteem Him. Surely He has borne our griefs and carried our sorrows; yet we esteemed Him stricken, smitten by God, and afflicted. But He was wounded for our transgressions, he was bruised for our iniquities; the chastisement for our peace was upon Him, and by His stripes we are healed. All we like sheep have gone astray; we have turned, every one, to his own way; and the LORD has laid on Him the iniquity of us all. He was oppressed and He was afflicted, yet He opened not His mouth; He was led as a lamb to the slaughter.
>
> Isaiah 53:3–7 (NKJV)

Jesus accomplished some great things for us when he shed his blood and died on the cross in our place. As we have discussed, his purpose was to restore us into a right relationship with God, but there are some added benefits to that which most of us are not even aware of.

First, it says he bore our griefs and carried our sorrows, and it also says that the chastisement of our peace was on him. In this life we lead here on earth, it is guaranteed that every one of us will face times of grief and sorrow. Jesus took all of that on himself and bore it for us. It doesn't mean we won't face difficult times, but when we do face them, we need to turn to Jesus. He'll walk through them with us, bringing comfort to our broken hearts and healing into our lives. The Bible also says, "and the peace of God, which surpasses all understanding, will guard your hearts and minds through Christ Jesus" (Philippians 4:7, NKJV). What more do we need in our lives and what is lacking more in this world than peace?

Then Isaiah tells us that Jesus was wounded for our transgressions and bruised for our iniquities. These are all the things we've done wrong and the bad choices we have made. Jesus paid the price for them so we don't have to.

Next, we are told that by his stripes we are healed. This is another thing every one of us, all of our friends, and all of our relatives will face: sickness, disease, and injury. The Bible tells us that Jesus was given thirty-nine stripes with a cat-o'-nine-tails. That was a horrible piece of equipment designed by the Romans to torture a man right to the point of death. Jesus took every one of those terrible stripes so our bodies could be healed from whatever ailment we might face.

One more thing his death did for us:

> Then Jesus shouted out again, and he gave up his spirit. At that moment the curtain in the Temple was torn in two, from top to bottom.
>
> Matthew 27:50,51 (NLT)

In the Old Testament only the high priest could go into the most holy place in the temple. It represented the very presence of God, his throne room. When Jesus died the curtain in front of that place was torn in two, split down the middle from the top to the bottom. What that signifies is access to God. Now through the shed blood of Jesus, his final sacrifice, everyone has access to God. You don't need a priest to go into God's throne room for you; you can go right on in there yourself! Anytime!

His Resurrection

This is when Jesus really kicked Satan in the teeth, or as we read earlier, "stepped on his head." When he was crucified, he shed his blood and died in our place so our sins could be forgiven, and we could be restored to a right relationship with God. When he rose from the dead, he completely defeated Satan and the power he had in this world.

> He who sins is of the devil, for the devil has sinned from the beginning. For this purpose the Son of God was manifested, that He might destroy the works of the devil.
>
> 1 John 3:8 (NKJV)

Satan really thought he was bringing about a major defeat to God and his plans for mankind when he had Jesus crucified. This really shows that Satan is not like God at all, and he has absolutely none of the godly attributes we read about in chapter two. He truly is a defeated foe with no power over any of our lives, unless we allow it. God allowed the crucifixion of Jesus, because it fulfilled his purpose of bringing us back into relationship with him.

> Then Pilate said to Him, "Are You not speaking to me? Do You not know that I have power to crucify You, and power to release You?"
>
> Jesus answered, "You could have no power at all against Me unless it had been given you from above. Therefore the one who delivered Me to you has the greater sin."
>
> John 19:10–11 (NKJV)

> But we speak the wisdom of God in a mystery, the hidden wisdom which God ordained before the ages for our glory, which none of the rulers of this age knew; for had they known, they would not have crucified the Lord of glory.
>
> 1 Corinthians 2:7–8 (NKJV)

These verses have a dual reference when it talks about the one who delivered Jesus to be crucified and the rulers of this age who didn't know what they were doing. It talks about the earthly men who were influenced by Satan to have Jesus killed, but the main object of these verses is Satan himself. He delivered Jesus to be crucified because he thought he was winning a war against God.

The Bible says that after Jesus died, he descended into the depths; took the keys of death, hell, and the grave away from Satan; and then released the righteous dead from paradise and then led them into heaven.

> When he ascended to the heights, he led a crowd of captives …
>
> Ephesians 4:8 (NLT)

> (Now this, "He ascended"—what does it mean but that He also first descended into the lower parts of the earth? He who descended is also the One who ascended far above all the heavens, that He might fill all things.)
>
> Ephesians 4:9 (NKJV)

> Having disarmed principalities and powers, He made a public spectacle of them, triumphing over them in it.
>
> Colossians 2:15 (NKJV)

> I am He who lives, and was dead, and behold, I am alive forevermore. Amen. And I have the keys of Hades and of Death.
>
> Revelation 1:18 (NKJV)

Let me explain what happened. Before Jesus came to earth and died for everyone's sin, there was a place that actually existed called Paradise. In Luke 16 Jesus called it Abraham's Bosom. It is probably where the Catholic concept of purgatory comes from. It was a holding place for all the people who served God but lived before the time of Jesus, those who were from the time of Adam, all the way up to the thief who died on the cross with Jesus. There were probably millions of them.

Since the only way to get to heaven is through Jesus, all of these people had to wait for him to die for their sins before they could get into heaven. So after he died, Jesus went and got them. First he had to go to Satan, take the keys away from him, and then go to the holding place and release the righteous people.

Then he released them from their holding place and led them into the very presence of God.

Can you picture Satan and his demonic forces? I'm sure they were having a party to celebrate their huge victory over Jesus. They had just killed the Son of God himself! I can see them jumping around, whooping and hollering, cheering, and making toasts to their great accomplishment. Suddenly Jesus walks into the room. The room goes deadly silent as he walks right up to Satan, takes the keys out of hands, then turns, and walks out without saying a word.

Then he goes to the holding place. A murmur starts as they see Jesus approaching, and it gets louder as they realize who he is and what he is doing. A mighty roar erupts as he opens the gates and leads them all into heaven. What a great day!

After that was all over, to really put Satan in his place and show him that he has no power over the Son of God, Jesus rose from the dead. By his resurrection, Jesus proved that death had no hold on him and that everything he had done and said while he was on earth was true. He truly is the Son of God; no one else has ever been able to raise himself from the dead.

Everyone in the history of the world has died and, once dead, stayed that way. It didn't matter how great they were in the eyes of man, they still died. All of the kings, queens, caesars, pharaohs, and presidents. All of the world's religious and political leaders, like Confucius, Buddha, Muhammad, Gandhi, George Washington, and Abraham Lincoln. Every pope, priest, bishop, and pastor. All of the celebrities, all of the famous, all of the infamous, every good guy, and every bad guy. They have all died, and every one of us will die. The Bible says:

> And as it is appointed for men to die once, but after this the judgment.
>
> Hebrews 9:27 (NKJV)

But it didn't apply to Jesus. He proved he was greater than all of them.

His Ascension

After Jesus rose from the dead, he spent forty days on earth visiting with and encouraging his followers. The Bible says that he was seen by over five hundred people during that time—over five hundred witnesses to his resurrected body. But at the end of the forty days, his closest followers went with him to a hill outside of Jerusalem called the Mount of Olives, where he was taken up into heaven.

> Now when He had spoken these things, while they watched, He was taken up, and a cloud received Him out of their sight. And while they looked steadfastly toward heaven as He went up, behold, two men stood by them in white apparel, who also said, "Men of Galilee, why do you stand gazing up into heaven? This same Jesus, who was taken up from you into heaven, will so come in like manner as you saw Him go into heaven."
>
> Acts 1:9–11 (NKJV)

> When the Lord Jesus had finished talking with them, he was taken up into heaven and sat down in the place of honor at God's right hand.
>
> Mark 16:19 (NKJV)

Most Christians do not realize it, but his ascension into heaven has had a huge impact on all of us. It changed everything.

> According to the working of His mighty power which He worked in Christ when He raised Him from the dead and seated Him at His right hand in the heavenly places, far above all principality and power and might and dominion, and every name that is named, not only in this age but also in that which is to come. And He put all things under His feet.
>
> Ephesians 1:19–22 (NKJV)

Jesus went up into heaven and is seated at the right hand of the Father with all principalities and powers under his feet. That is speaking of Satan and his demonic kingdom; they are under the feet of Jesus. They have no power over Jesus, and he has total control over them. That all sounds nice, doesn't it? But you're probably asking, "What does that have to do with me?" Look at this verse from the very next chapter of Ephesians.

> But God, who is rich in mercy, because of His great love with which He loved us, even when we were dead in trespasses, made us alive together with Christ (by grace you have been saved), and

> raised us up together, and made us sit together in the heavenly places in Christ Jesus.
>
> Ephesians 2:4–6 (NKJV)

See what that says? We are sitting there right beside him! We have been raised up together and sit together in heaven with Jesus. That might be a little hard for us to understand; we know that physically we can see where we are right now, and we probably don't see Jesus anywhere around. But in the spirit world, things are very different. As I have said before, we don't really comprehend it. I know, though, that this verse tells me my position as a Christian is sitting with Jesus at the right hand of the Father with all principalities and powers under *my* feet. They have no power over me either. Satan and his demonic forces are under my feet. What a great place for him to be.

Making It Mine

God came to earth and did all of these things just for you. Not accepting them or doing anything with them is kind of like having a billion dollars in the bank and never using any of it. Most of us really have no idea how to make all of this part of our life and not sure why we need to or if we even want to.

Some of us have misconceptions about what it takes or what it means to be Christian. We might think, *America is a Christian nation, right? So we're all Christians, and if we're good, we'll all go to heaven.* Others might say, "I go to church," or "I'm a Presbyterian," or "I'm a Catholic." Some think that it really doesn't matter what you believe as long as you believe something. But remember what Jesus said?

> Jesus said to him, "I am the way, the truth, and the life. No one comes to the Father except through Me."
>
> John 14:6 (NKJV)

Jesus says that he is the only way to God. How do you go through Jesus to get to God? What does that mean? How do you make all of this stuff part of your life?

> Jesus answered and said to him, "Most assuredly, I say to you, unless you are born again, you cannot see the Kingdom of God."
>
> John 3:3 (NKJV)

Remember we talked about God being a spirit and living in a spiritual world and about us being a spirit too. That spiritual world is where all of this takes place. Our relationship with God will take place in our spirits. Because of sin in the world, our spirit has no connection with God. It was designed to be connected, so it needs to be reconnected. That is what Jesus called being born again. Our physical body was born at our physical birth, and now we need to have a spiritual birth. So how do we make that happen?

> That if you confess with your mouth the Lord Jesus and believe in your heart that God has raised Him from the dead, you will be saved.
>
> Romans 10:9 (NKJV)

What does that say? Basically this: believe that all of this information I have been sharing with you about Jesus is true. Believe he is the Son of God and believe that God raised him from the dead. Then make the conscious decision to accept him and follow him. That's it! That's all! There's nothing else!

If you are willing and you want to establish this relationship with God, pray this prayer with me now: *Lord Jesus, I believe you are the Son of God. I believe that God raised you from the dead. Come into my life right now and establish that relationship with me that I was designed for. Thank you for loving me, and forgiving me, and accepting me just the way I am.*

That's all there is to it. If you prayed that prayer and meant it, then you are now in a right relationship with God; your spirit has been reconnected to his spirit. Congratulations, it is the best and most important decision you will ever make. He is going to start doing some great things in your life.

> Being confident of this very thing, that He who has begun a good work in you will complete it until the day of Jesus Christ.
>
> Philippians 1:6 (NKJV)

The Stages of Being Saved

You will hear different terms in most churches for the born-again experience that we have just been talking about and you just experienced. The three I've heard used the most are: saved, born again, and asking Jesus into your heart. Probably the most common is being saved. We are saved from a life of death and destruction and spending eternity separated from God. The one that is probably used most often in a setting with children is asking Jesus into your heart. The implication here is turning your life over to Jesus and letting him live his life through you. Then of course, born again, which is the term Jesus used to explain our spirit being reconnected to God's spirit as it was originally designed. All three refer to the same event but have just a slightly different implication for what took place. All three are correct and are basically interchangeable.

What might come as a surprise to some, however, is that being saved is actually a three-stage process we all have to go through.

We learned in chapter two that we are actually made up of three parts: the spirit, soul, and body. What we probably didn't realize is that each one of those parts is saved in a different way.

The Spirit

This is where it all begins. The other parts cannot get saved if this one doesn't. The second you make the decision to accept Jesus and what he has done for you, your spirit is saved; it is as saved as it is ever going to be. You are as saved as Billy Graham or the Apostle Paul. There is nothing you can do to make yourself more saved. There is also nothing you can do to make yourself less saved. Basically all you need to do now is believe it, accept it, and walk in it.

> Therefore, if anyone is in Christ, he is a new creation; old things have passed away; behold, all things have become new.
>
> 2 Corinthians 5:17 (NKJV)

You are a brand-new creation, not at all the same as you used to be. All of your old life is behind you, and a new life is laid out before you, just waiting for you to discover all God has for you. Here are some biblical and theological words that describe what just happened to you.

1. *Atonement.* When you commit a crime, you have to pay for it. Our sinful lives have to be paid for too. This word comes from the Old Testament when animals were used to make atonement for the sins of the people. Jesus came and made atonement for your sins. He paid the price so you don't have to.
2. *Justification.* A judicial term meaning to acquit. You have been declared innocent. Remember it this way, "Just as if I had never sinned." The Bible says that because of the shed blood of Jesus, God looks at us as though we are righteous. Notice that is not based on anything we do or have ever done; it is based on what Jesus did.
3. *Redemption.* To pay the price in order to buy something back that belonged to you in the first place. When a valuable object of yours is lost or stolen, you will do whatever it takes to find it. When you locate it, you will pay whatever the asking price to regain possession of it. God created us, and we belonged to him; then he lost us. Then Jesus came and bought us back; now we belong to God again.

4. *Reconciliation.* It means brought back into relationship. God's desire has always been for us to have a daily relationship with him. When that relationship was destroyed, he came after us and made it possible for the relationship to be restored. When we accepted Jesus, the reconciliation actually took place.
5. *Regeneration.* Even though we are spirit beings, before we are born again our spirit is almost in a dormant state. It is where our life comes from, but it is unaware of spiritual things and has no comprehension of the spirit world. When we are born spiritually, it is as though we are being created for the first time. Now our spirit is suddenly alive and has some say in how we live our lives. Our spirit is how we are connected to God, and the more we let our spirit control how we live, the more we will change and grow in our spiritual walk.
6. *Propitiation.* This unusual word is found in the book of 1 John, and it means to break down the barrier. Sin separated us from God, and it was a barrier that stood between us. By coming and dying in our place and paying for our sins, Jesus removed that barrier and allowed us to come back to God. Jesus was the propitiation that paid the price, broke down the barrier, and restored our relationship with God.
7. *Sanctification.* This means to be set apart. God came and restored us back into a relationship with him; then he set us apart. We have been set aside to be used by God, however he sees fit. God had

a purpose and a plan for creating you and for putting you right here, right now.

> Yet who knows whether you have come to the kingdom for such a time as this?
>
> Esther 4:13 (NKJV)

In order for you to fulfill that plan, God is going to develop you into the person he needs you to be.

> The Lord directs the steps of the godly. He delights in every detail of their lives.
>
> Psalm 37:23 (NLT)

The thing about God is that in all of your developing and all of your growing, he will be using you for his purposes all along the way. So submit yourself to God and his leadership for your life and watch the great things he will do with you.

The Soul

If we were to die at any time after we are born again spiritually, both our spirit and our soul would go to heaven. They are eternally connected; you can't have one without the other. Remember that our souls are the place where we really live. It is our thoughts and feelings toward life. It is how we have learned to think, and believe, and react, over a lifetime of circumstances and decisions. All of that doesn't change overnight. We might be Christians now, but we have spent our entire lives developing who we are up to this point of our existence. This is going to take some time to change.

Most new Christians will doubt their born-again experience in the first few days and weeks after it happens. We come to the realization that nothing has really changed, at least physically, in our lives. We are still living in the same house, with the same spouse, in the same marriage, with the same kids and the same job. We begin to think, *How could I have been so foolish to believe such a bunch nonsense. That was obviously just a silly, emotional decision I just made. I need to come back down to earth and get back to reality. Nothing is ever really going to change in my life.*

The reason we think thoughts like that is: while our spirits were changed instantly when we accepted Jesus, our souls have a process to go through that takes a lifetime. Paul says we have to change the way we think.

> Don't copy the behavior and customs of this world, but let God transform you into a new person by changing the way you think. Then you will learn to know God's will for you, which is good and pleasing and perfect.
>
> Romans 12:2 (NLT)

This is how our souls get saved, and we'll devote all of chapter seven to this process, because this is where the rubber meets the road. This is where we go from just calling ourselves Christians to actually living like a Christian. This is where we learn to set aside the things that are holding us back in life and move into the design and destiny that God had in mind for us from the beginning.

The Body

Unfortunately, as you have probably noticed by now, your body didn't change when you were born again. Sure, now you can learn to make better choices, and maybe you can take care of your body a little better. But many people who will never have anything to do with God take good care of their bodies. No matter what we do, our bodies continue to deteriorate. Sometimes it feels as if we are falling apart right before our own eyes. The Bible has a great promise for us.

> It is the same way with the resurrection of the dead. Our earthly bodies are planted in the ground when we die, but they will be raised to live forever. Our bodies are buried in brokenness, but they will be raised in glory. They are buried in weakness, but they will be raised in strength. They are buried as natural human bodies, but they will be raised as spiritual bodies. For just as there are natural bodies, there are also spiritual bodies.
>
> 1 Corinthians 15:42–44 (NLT)

> But we are citizens of heaven, where the Lord Jesus Christ lives. And we are eagerly waiting for him to return as our Savior. He will take our weak mortal bodies and change them into glorious bodies like his own, using the same power with which he will bring everything under his control.
>
> Philippians 3:20–21 (NLT)

Our bodies will get saved when Jesus comes back. Then we are going to get brand-new bodies that will never get sick and never die, the same kind that Adam and Eve had before the fall and the kind that Jesus had as he appeared on earth in the forty days after his resurrection, a body that is in the prime of life that will never age, be overweight, or get out of shape, one that will never suffer from disease, injury, or disability. Sounds exciting, doesn't it? I can't wait.

Two Ordinances

Before Jesus went back to heaven, he left us with two ceremonies, called ordinances, that symbolize what he did for us when he came to earth, died on the cross, rose from the dead, and restored our relationship to God. As Christians, we are asked to observe these ordinances to remember what Jesus did for us. We willingly take part in them out of obedience to Jesus, just because he asked us to.

Baptism in water

After we are born again, Jesus tells us we need to be baptized in water.

> Go therefore and make disciples of all the nations, baptizing them in the name of the Father and of the Son and of the Holy Spirit.
>
> Matthew 28:19 (NKJV)

The Greek word translated *baptism* actually means to immerse in water or to make fully wet. So after we are saved, we are to take the step of being fully immersed in water. Our salvation comes through faith in Jesus, so baptism has nothing to do with our salvation. It is simply an act of obedience to the command of Jesus.

The act of being dunked under water during baptism symbolizes Jesus dying and being buried, and then coming up out of the water symbolizes Jesus being raised from the dead and coming up out of the grave.

It also symbolizes what has taken place in our lives when we become born again. When we go under the water, it symbolizes our old sinful nature being put to death, and then we come out of the water and rise to a new life in Jesus.

Before Jesus started his ministry, he was baptized in water, and all through the book of Acts are stories of new believers being baptized in water. Most were baptized almost immediately after they accepted Jesus. After we are saved, we also need to be baptized, but there are no requirements on timing. It just needs to be done after you are born again. If you haven't been baptized yet, ask your pastor when is the next time your church will be holding a baptismal service and get signed up. It's important for you to take that step, and you'll be glad you did.

Communion

As Jesus was eating the Last Supper with his disciples, he instituted the ordinance of communion. It is recorded in the books of Matthew, Mark, and Luke. Later, Paul wrote a letter to the people in Corinth;

there he gave them some instructions on communion and told the story again. Here is how he recorded it:

> For I received from the Lord that which I also delivered to you: that the Lord Jesus on the same night in which He was betrayed took bread; and when He had given thanks, He broke it and said, "Take, eat; this is My body which is broken for you; do this in remembrance of Me."
>
> In the same manner He also took the cup after supper, saying, "This cup is the new covenant in My blood. This do, as often as you drink it, in remembrance of Me."
>
> For as often as you eat this bread and drink this cup, you proclaim the Lord's death till He comes.
>
> 1 Corinthians 11:23–27 (NKJV)

The bread represents the body of Jesus that was broken for us, and the cup represents his blood that was shed for us. He said they represent the New Covenant that God made with man when Jesus came and died for our sins. Jesus said to take them in remembrance of himself.

Neither Paul nor Jesus told us how often to take communion. They just said, "whenever you do." Some churches have communion every week, while others only take it once a month. It really doesn't matter. There is no time frame or occasion when we are required to take communion. We are just asked to do it.

The one stipulation that Paul put on it is that we have to be worthy.

> So anyone who eats this bread or drinks this cup of the Lord unworthily is guilty of sinning against the body and blood of the Lord. That is why you should examine yourself before eating the bread and drinking the cup. For if you eat the bread or drink the cup without honoring the body of Christ, you are eating and drinking God's judgment upon yourself. That is why many of you are weak and sick and some have even died. But if we would examine ourselves, we would not be judged by God in this way. Yet when we are judged by the Lord, we are being disciplined so that we will not be condemned along with the world.
>
> 1 Corinthians 11:27–32 (NKJV)

Taking communion unworthily is taking it with obvious sin in our lives. That is why we are supposed to examine ourselves. When communion is served, we should take the time to search ourselves for things we might be doing wrong. We should ask the Holy Spirit to show us things in our life that need to be corrected. When he reveals them to us, we ask for his forgiveness and then ask for his help to change. Then we can go ahead and take communion. It is an awesome opportunity God gives us to give our lives a check up once in a while. Those verses we just read say that if we are willing to examine ourselves and make changes when they are revealed to us, then we don't have to face God's judgment. Sounds like a pretty good deal to me.

Conclusion

We talked in the last chapter about eternal separation from God that we were not designed for. Let's talk about eternal life with God that we were designed for.

If we have accepted Jesus and are in a committed relationship with God, we do not even have to appear at the Great White Throne Judgment, that place where everyone in the history of the world who died without accepting Jesus will get to stand trial in front of God. After our life on earth is over we will appear at the judgment seat of Christ instead. At this judgment you will answer for your life on earth too, not whether you accepted Jesus or not, but how faithful you were with what was given to you and what was required of you. Eternity in heaven or hell is not in the balance, just the kind and amount of rewards you will receive for your obedience and faithfulness in serving God.

> So we are always confident, knowing that while we are at home in the body we are absent from the Lord. For we walk by faith, not by sight. We are confident, yes, well pleased rather to be absent from the body and to be present with the Lord. Therefore we make it our aim, whether present or absent, to be well pleasing to Him. For we must all appear before the Judgment Seat of Christ, that each one may receive the things done in the body, according to what he has done, whether good or bad.
>
> 2 Corinthians 5:6–10 (NKJV)

> Each one's work will become clear; for the Day will declare it, because it will be revealed by fire; and the fire will test each one's work, of what sort it is. If anyone's work which he has built on it endures, he will receive a reward. If anyone's work is burned, he will suffer loss; but he himself will be saved, yet so as through fire.
>
> 1 Corinthians 3:13–15 (NKJV)

There are many descriptions in the Bible of what eternity with God is like. Here are just a few of them. Listen to how wonderful they sound: my Father's house, the Promised Land, the marriage supper, the fullness of joy, the fullness of knowledge, and a place of rest. It sounds great, doesn't it? I've got some bad news for you, though, if you were planning on earning your wings and becoming an angel in heaven. The angels were created to be angels; you weren't. You are going to be you, just as you are now, only better. Heaven is going to be a place where we are busy with service to the Lord, a place where we have friends and family around us continually, and a place of happiness and laughter.

If the only reason for serving God were the option of spending eternity with God or eternity separated from God, it would be ridiculous for you to choose separation. If the odds were a million to one that any of the subject matter I am laying out for you in this book is true, you would be a complete fool to not believe it.

God created you to know, love, and serve him in this present world and to enjoy him forever in the world to come. Don't miss out on all he has for you.

Our Helper

> "But you will receive power when the Holy Spirit comes upon you. And you will be my witnesses, telling people about me everywhere—in Jerusalem, throughout Judea, in Samaria, and to the ends of the earth."
>
> Acts 1:8 (NKJV)

Principle 6 – As Christians we believe that it is the Holy Spirit who gives us the power to live victorious lives, to share our faith with others, and to impact the world around us.

After Jesus went back to heaven, the Holy Spirit became the part of the Godhead that presides over our lives. In the Old Testament, God the Father was the primary way God revealed himself to man. Then Jesus, the Son of God, came to earth and resided with us for thirty-three years. He accomplished his mission to restore mankind back to God and defeat the works of Satan. When he returned to heaven, he sent the Holy Spirit to us, to walk with us, to take care of us, to guide us, and to strengthen us.

> Nevertheless I tell you the truth. It is to your advantage that I go away; for if I do not go away,

> the Helper will not come to you; but if I depart, I will send Him to you. And when He has come, He will convict the world of sin, and of righteousness, and of judgment: of sin, because they do not believe in Me; of righteousness, because I go to My Father and you see Me no more; of judgment, because the ruler of this world is judged. I still have many things to say to you, but you cannot bear them now, however when He, the Spirit of truth, has come, He will guide you into all truth; for He will not speak on His own authority, but whatever He hears He will speak; and He will tell you things to come. He will glorify Me, for He will take of what is Mine and declare it to you. All things that the Father has are Mine. Therefore I said that He will take of Mine and declare it to you.
>
> John 16:7–15 (NKJV)

Now, when we talk to God, we are talking to the Holy Spirit. He is not some obscure, ghostly figure, with a shadowy existence. He is God, with all of the godly names and attributes we talked about in chapter two. Jesus called him our Helper, and he is available to us, to walk with, and talk with, and to spend our days with.

The Biblical Description of the Holy Spirit

When the Bible talks about the Holy Spirit, it uses a different way of explaining him to us than was used to teach us about the Father or the Son. The Holy Spirit is described by using symbols. These symbols provide us with a word picture of what the Holy Spirit does in our lives when we accept Jesus and walk in a relationship with God.

Fire

The flame of a fire produces both heat and light. It can completely destroy something by reducing it to ashes, or it can be used to cleanse a valuable material by destroying its impurities. The symbol of *fire* represents the cleansing and purifying power of the Holy Spirit.

> John answered, saying to all, "I indeed baptize you with water; but One mightier than I is coming, whose sandal strap I am not worthy to loose. He will baptize you with the Holy Spirit and fire."
>
> Luke 3:16 (NKJV)

The Holy Spirit purges us of sin and purifies us so we can be used by God. Then he gives us a boldness and zeal to step out and minister to others in the name of Jesus.

Wind

Wind is an invisible movement of air that can be gentle and refreshing or powerful and destructive. The symbol of *wind* represents the mysterious and independent will of the Holy Spirit.

> The wind blows where it wishes, and you hear the sound of it, but cannot tell where it comes from

> and where it goes. So is everyone who is born of the Spirit.
>
> John 3:8 (NKJV)

> And suddenly there came a sound from heaven, as of a rushing mighty wind, and it filled the whole house where they were sitting.
>
> Acts 2:2 (NKJV)

The Holy Spirit moves around mysteriously wherever and whenever he chooses. He penetrates into the very depths of our beings and gives life.

Water

Water is a clear, colorless, odorless, and tasteless liquid that can be used for cleaning, cooling, or to satisfy our thirst. The symbol of *water* represents the cleansing and refreshing power of the Holy Spirit.

> Then I will sprinkle clean water on you, and you will be clean. Your filth will be washed away, and you will no longer worship idols. And I will give you a new heart with new and right desires, and I will put a new spirit in you. I will take out your stony heart of sin and give you a new, obedient heart. And I will put my Spirit in you so you will obey my laws and do whatever I command.
>
> Ezekiel 36:25–27 (NLT)

> On the last day, that great day of the feast, Jesus stood and cried out, saying, "If anyone thirsts, let him come to Me and drink. He who believes in Me, as the Scripture has said, out of his heart will flow rivers of living water." But this He spoke

> concerning the Spirit, whom those believing in Him would receive; for the Holy Spirit was not yet given, because Jesus was not yet glorified.
>
> John 7:37–39 (NKJV)

The Holy Spirit quenches our thirst; he cleanses, refreshes, and strengthens us. He is like a deep and flowing river, and the deeper we go into the water, the more we let go of our own will and allow his strength to flow through us, the more he can accomplish with us.

A Seal

A seal is a stamp or emblem used to signify ownership, authenticity, and trust. The symbol of the *seal* represents ownership and security.

> In Him you also trusted, after you heard the word of truth, the gospel of your salvation; in whom also, having believed, you were sealed with the Holy Spirit of promise, who is the guarantee of our inheritance until the redemption of the purchased possession, to the praise of His glory.
>
> Ephesians 1:13–14 (NKJV)

This is like an ancient king putting his seal on an official document. It told everyone who saw it that this was the word of the king and they better pay attention. The Holy Spirit has placed his seal on us. This is our guarantee that we belong to him, that everything he has promised will come true, and everyone (including Satan) needs to pay attention. This is a child of the King.

Oil

Throughout the Bible are stories and examples of the use of oil. It is used when anointing someone to hold an office, like priest or king, as a healing balm to restore health to the sick or injured and as fuel for light and heating. The symbol of *oil* represents the authority, the usefulness, the healing, illuminating, liberating power of the Holy Spirit.

> Then Samuel took the horn of oil and anointed him in the midst of his brothers; and the Spirit of the LORD came upon David from that day forward.
>
> 1 Samuel 16:13 (NKJV)

David was anointed to be king, and when the oil was poured over him, he received the power of the Holy Spirit.

> And you know that God anointed Jesus of Nazareth with the Holy Spirit and with power. Then Jesus went around doing good and healing all who were oppressed by the devil, for God was with him.
>
> Acts 10:38 (NLT)

In the same way David was anointed with oil, Jesus was anointed with the Holy Spirit and with power.

> But the anointing which you have received from Him abides in you, and you do not need that anyone teach you; but as the same anointing teaches you concerning all things.
>
> 1 John 2:27 (NKJV)

We have the same anointing, the same Holy Spirit, and the same power operating in our lives that

David and Jesus had. When someone was anointed with oil, it spoke of a transfer of power, of usefulness, and of fruitfulness. Oil was applied to wounds, and it brought soothing and healing to the injury. It is used to fuel fires for warmth and illumination and to bring lubrication to mechanical objects.

The Holy Spirit does all of those things in our lives. He gives us power to live both useful and fruitful lives. He brings soothing and healing to the wounds we receive just by living in our own cruel and hard circumstances. He illuminates our paths by teaching us about the ways of God and brings the comfort of warmth in the coldness we face every day. He loosens and liberates us as we are given freedom from the ways of this world and freedom to move in the power of the Holy Spirit.

The Dove

The dove is a peaceful, gentle bird with a soft cooing call. The symbol of the *dove* represents peace, gentleness, patience, and meekness.

> When He had been baptized, Jesus came up immediately from the water; and behold, the heavens were opened to Him, and He saw the Spirit of God descending like a dove and alighting upon Him.
>
> Matthew 3:16 (NKJV)

The Holy Spirit is a quiet gentleman, and he never forces his way into our lives. He has all the power of the God that spoke the universe into existence, but he allows us to run our own lives the way we want to. If we were to let him in and allow him to run things, we would see ourselves with gentleness and peace in our lives instead of the constant turmoil we face now.

The Functions of the Holy Spirit

The Conviction of the Holy Spirit

Before we accept Jesus, the Holy Spirit is always after us. God loves us so much that he will never give up on us.

> But if I depart, I will send Him to you. And when He has come, He will convict the world of sin, and of righteousness, and of judgment: of sin, because they do not believe in Me; of righteousness, because I go to My Father and you see Me no more; of judgment, because the ruler of this world is judged.
>
> John 16:7–11 (NKJV)

The word *convict* used in this verse means to let us know that the things we are doing are not right and to show us that there is a better way to live. The Holy Spirit's role is to reveal Jesus to a lost and dying world and to let us know that Jesus is the answer to all of the problems we face in life.

It doesn't matter where we go, what we do, how much we laugh and ridicule, how mean and hard we are, or how much we resist; he will always be right there. He wants to give us all the opportunity to accept

Jesus, so he will always be arranging ways for that to happen. He will put us in situations where we hear the message, he will put people in our paths that bring the message to us, and he will speak to our hearts and remind us that there is a better way and we need to make a change. When we reject him and push him away, he doesn't lose interest and give up on us.

He loves you totally and completely. He wants you to let him into your heart and let him be a part of your life every day. He will never give up on you. He will stay after you until the very last second you are alive.

If you have made the decision to be born again, it was no accident. It wasn't coincidence that someone crossed your path who would explain Jesus to you. It wasn't a stroke of luck that you picked up this book to read it, and it wasn't fate that arranged the events of your life in order to bring you into a church that gave you the opportunity to accept Jesus. Whatever your story might have been (we all have one) that brought you to the place and the time when you came to the realization that you needed Jesus, the Holy Spirit arranged it. As a matter of fact, it would have been impossible for you to get saved if the Holy Spirit had not been working.

The Indwelling of the Holy Spirit

Now that you've taken the step to allow Jesus into your life and to reestablish your relationship with God, the Holy Spirit is living inside of you.

> He is the Holy Spirit, who leads into all truth. The world cannot receive him, because it isn't looking

> for him and doesn't recognize him. But you know him, because he lives with you now and later will be in you.
>
> John 14:17 (NLT)

> The Spirit of God, who raised Jesus from the dead, lives in you. And just as he raised Christ from the dead, he will give life to your mortal body by this same Spirit living within you.
>
> Romans 8:11 (NLT)

> Or don't you know that your body is the temple of the Holy Spirit, who lives in you and was given to you by God? You do not belong to yourself.
>
> 1 Corinthians 6:19 (NLT)

He is there to walk with you through your everyday life. He is there to guide and direct our lives if we are willing to listen.

> When the Spirit of truth comes, he will guide you into all truth.
>
> John16:13 (NLT)

When we become Christians, the Holy Spirit begins to work in our life. Since our spirit has now been regenerated, we now have a spiritual connection with God, and he is able to talk to us and show us things we need to do and changes we need to make. Our conscience becomes rejuvenated, and the Holy Spirit will use that to let us know when we are making bad choices and heading in the wrong direction.

Some of the changes we need to make will be easy and will almost seem to happen automatically. Others might be harder and take more of an effort to bring about. We're all different, and it doesn't happen the same for any of us. For example, some people with bad habits like smoking, drinking, or drugs will see them drop off almost immediately. Others will have a more difficult time and might struggle for months or even years. And there are many things we might need to change: lying, stealing, sexual sins, anger, abuse, jealousy, and bad language, just to name a few. The list is endless, with as many variations as there are people. In our early days as a new Christian, our bad behaviors seem to fall away quickly, but over time it gets a little harder. When our more obvious problems start to disappear, the Holy Spirit begins to work on our hidden sins, our attitudes, our motivations, our rebelliousness, and the secret things we do when no one else is looking.

We have been living our entire lives up to the point we got saved with our souls in charge. Remember, that is the way we think, the feelings we have, and our willpower. When you become a Christian, your spirit has been rejuvenated and is now connected with God. It is a major step for us to take when we go from being a soul-led person to a spirit-led person. Our souls are pretty stubborn and won't want to give up the leadership position easily. A lot of new Christians will do well for a while; but when the choices get harder and the changes become more of a challenge, they might end up taking a few steps backwards, and some will walk away altogether.

The Holy Spirit is the one who brings about the

changes in our lives. In the early days of our Christianity, the changes were taking place so easily, and things were going so well we thought it would just continue on like that forever. But the Holy Spirit is a gentleman. Even though you are now a Christian, he is still not going to impose his will on you. He is not going to force you to make the changes you need to make. You will have to make a conscious choice to ask for his help and then make the decision to be obedient to his leading.

Here is a prayer that you can pray right now to ask for his help: *Holy Spirit, thank you for coming and living inside of me and becoming an active part of my life. Help me follow you as you lead me, guide me, and direct my steps through life. Cause me to be aware of your presence in my life, to hear your voice when you speak to me about the changes I need to make, and to be obedient to your leading. Help me allow you to set the direction for my life and to be willing to follow your guidance. I ask this in Jesus's name, amen.*

The Holy Spirit is always guiding us and directing our lives. The problem is, we're just not always listening. Taking the step to invite him to lead and asking his help in obeying is actually more of a step for us to be willing to pay attention.

It is very important for us to live a Holy Spirit-led life. We will never make it on our own; he is the only one that can lead us to a victorious Christian life.

Jesus promised us a good life. He said, "I have come that they may have life, and that they may have it more abundantly" (John 10:10, NKJV).

You don't have to wait until your life is a struggle

to pray that prayer. It would be good to do it before you mess your life up, but most of us are not that smart. We need to get ourselves in a bind doing things our own way before we are willing to ask for help. If your life does seem hard and anything but the abundant life Jesus promised, then go back and say that prayer right now and learn to live a Holy Spirit-led life. You will be glad you did, and you will be amazed at the change.

The Fruit of the Spirit

When we accept Jesus and are spiritually reborn, the Holy Spirit begins to work in our lives. He challenges us to make the changes necessary to live the kind of prosperous and successful life that will impact the world around us. The extent to which we are willing to listen and willing to make the changes as he reveals them to us will determine how far we advance in the kingdom of God and how much he is able to use us. When we are listening to the Holy Spirit and changing, it becomes evident in our lives that change is taking place. The Bible calls that evidence the fruit of the spirit.

> But the Fruit of the Spirit is love, joy, peace, patience, kindness, goodness, faithfulness, gentleness and self-control. Against such things there is no law.
>
> Galatians 5:22–23 (NKJV)

When we observe the behavior of Christians, we should be able to see these fruits in action. We are all a work in progress and at different stages of development, but we all should see these fruits growing in our lives. If you notice a Christian you are acquainted with fall short in some of these areas from time to time, don't judge them. Just realize that they are under construction just as you are. When you see a Christian who seems so calm and easy going and you wonder how anybody could be that cheerful and easy to get along with, remember it is the Holy Spirit working in our lives and our willingness to change that allows the fruit to be evident.

The Baptism of the Holy Spirit

This is an area of such controversy in the Christian community that I contemplated leaving it out altogether. I know, however, that this should be a very important part of every Christian's life, and for that reason I can't avoid the issue just because it might cause a little uneasiness. There are as many opinions about this subject as there are Christian denominations and churches. It has caused more division in the body of Christ than anything I know of. As I was praying and thinking about this and asking God how to handle it, I decided that the only thing I can really do is explain it to you the way I have been taught and the way I believe it.

I also don't want to have this section cause people to not read this book at all, because I think it is very important for all believers to have at least a basic understanding of Christian theology and how it applies to our everyday lives. If nothing else, I will at least be able to give a little insight on how most Pentecostal churches believe. Even here though, there are differences among the Pentecostal groups in how they believe and how they put their beliefs into practice. All I can tell you is, if you belong to a denomination or go to a church that believes differently than I do, then go to your leaders and ask them to explain how and why they believe what they do.

Earlier we talked about the indwelling of the Holy Spirit, and many churches end their teachings on the purposes of the Holy Spirit right there. Some take one more step and say a prayer similar to the one I had you pray earlier in this chapter, and they would call that being filled with the Spirit. The problem with that, I think, is that the Holy Spirit is living inside every one of us the minute we accept Jesus. All we have to do is learn to listen and obey.

The baptism of the Holy Spirit is something completely different. You can tell by the words the Bible uses to describe it. Two words in particular tell me that there is more to it than just living a good Christian life. Those words are *fire* and *power.* To me, that makes it sound quite a bit more exciting and a lot more intense than just being good. There's nothing wrong with being good; hopefully we are all growing and maturing and becoming better each day. But I think the Holy Spirit has even more for you. Are you ready? Are you willing? If you are, the Holy Spirit will take you, transform you, and utilize you to change the world.

Before Jesus started his ministry, John the Baptist prophesied that there was one coming after him

(Jesus) who would baptize with the Holy Spirit and with fire.

> John answered, saying to all, "I indeed baptize you with water; but One mightier than I is coming, whose sandal strap I am not worthy to loose. He will baptize you with the Holy Spirit and fire."
>
> Luke 3:16 (NKJV)

Then, right before Jesus went back to heaven, he told his disciples to go back to Jerusalem and wait for the Holy Spirit.

> But you shall receive power when the Holy Spirit has come upon you; and you shall be witnesses to Me in Jerusalem, and in all Judea and Samaria, and to the end of the earth.
>
> Acts 1:8 (NKJV)

He promised them that when the Holy Spirit came upon them they would have power. That is what the baptism of the Holy Spirit is all about, power. It is the power to live such a victorious Christian life that it impacts the lives of others, and it is using that power of the Holy Spirit to minister to the needs of the people around you.

When a person receives the baptism of the Holy Spirit, the evidence that it has taken place is that the person will speak in tongues. This is pretty scary to a lot of people, and a lot of people question it, but it is what the Bible says. I don't know why many people believe the entire Bible and then take this part and decide it isn't true or doesn't apply to today. There is nothing about it we should be afraid of. It's only speaking in another language; it's just that when you speak in this language you have no idea what you are saying. It is not a language that you know or understand. The Holy Spirit gives you the words to say.

There are five occasions in the book of Acts when people are baptized in the Holy Spirit. In each case, speaking in tongues is either specifically mentioned or implied.

1. The first time is at the very beginning of the early church on the day of Pentecost. *Pentecost* is a Greek word that means *fifty*. It was a Jewish holiday that took place fifty days after the Passover.

> When the Day of Pentecost had fully come, they were all with one accord in one place. And suddenly there came a sound from heaven, as of a rushing mighty wind, and it filled the whole house where they were sitting. Then there appeared to them divided tongues, as of fire, and one sat upon each of them. And they were all filled with the Holy Spirit and began to speak with other tongues, as the Spirit gave them utterance.
>
> Acts 2:1–4 (NKJV)

This was the day Jesus had told his followers to wait for. It says that when they were filled with the Holy Spirit they all began to speak in other tongues. When you continue on with the story, you will find out that they were indeed filled with power just as Jesus had promised them. The Bible says a large crowd began to gather because of the commotion and that Peter stood up to preach and explained to all of them about Jesus. Three thousand people got saved that day! You talk about power!

2. The next time the Bible says that people spoke in tongues took place when Peter was summoned to the home of a commander in the Roman army named Cornelius. The Bible says he was a devout man and that an angel appeared to him and told him to send for Peter. A large gathering was waiting for Peter when he arrived, so he began to explain to them all about Jesus and what he had done for them.

> While Peter was still speaking these words, the Holy Spirit fell upon all those who heard the word. And those of the circumcision who believed were astonished, as many as came with Peter, because the gift of the Holy Spirit had been poured out on the Gentiles also. For they heard them speak with tongues and magnify God.
>
> Acts 10:44–46 (NKJV)

So while Peter was still preaching to them, the Holy Spirit fell on all of them, and they were baptized in the Holy Spirit. How did Peter and his friends know that they had received the Holy Spirit? Because they all spoke in tongues.

3. Then, when Paul first arrived in the city of Ephesus, he came across a group of men who had apparently been baptized by John the Baptist. Paul explained to them about Jesus, the one John came to introduce to the world. They accepted Jesus and were baptized in water; then Paul laid hands on them, and they were baptized in the Holy Spirit.

> And when Paul had laid hands on them, the Holy Spirit came upon them, and they spoke with tongues and prophesied.
>
> Acts 19:6 (NKJV)

Once again we read that when they received the Holy Spirit they spoke in tongues, and this time they prophesied too.

4. Then we have the time when the Apostle Paul himself was baptized in the Holy Spirit. His Hebrew name was Saul, and in Greek his name was Paul. So here he is called Saul, and later when he became a minister to the Gentiles, he became known as Paul. Before he was saved, Saul was one of those who persecuted the Christians. One day, as Saul was traveling to Damascus to capture and imprison more of the believers, Jesus appeared to him in a bright light and knocked him off his donkey. Saul was blinded by the light, but from that point forward he was a believer in Jesus. His men took him into town, and God sent one of his followers, a man named Ananias, to pray for him.

> And Ananias went his way and entered the house; and laying his hands on him he said, "Brother Saul, the Lord Jesus, who appeared to you on the road as you came, has sent me that you may receive your sight and be filled with the Holy Spirit." Immediately there fell from his eyes something like scales, and he received his sight at once; and he arose and was baptized.
>
> Acts 9:17–18 (NKJV)

This time speaking in tongues is implied. It says that Ananias prayed for him to be filled with Holy Spirit and to be healed. It doesn't say that he spoke in tongues, but it does say he was healed. The implication comes later in a letter Paul wrote to the church in Corinth when he talked about speaking in tongues.

> I thank God that I speak in tongues more than all of you.
>
> 1 Corinthians 14:18 (NLT)

Here, Paul seems to be bragging about how much he speaks in tongues. He isn't really bragging; it comes in the middle of a teaching he is doing on the gifts of the Spirit that we will cover a little bit later. The point is that he spoke in tongues. When do you suppose he started to speak in tongues? I think it is logical to assume that he began to speak in tongues when he was prayed for by Ananias to be filled with the Holy Spirit.

5. Then there was an incident that took place when a great persecution broke out against the Christians. Many of them left Jerusalem and began to spread out into other areas and countries seeking safety. One of the disciples, a man named Philip, went to Samaria and started to preach there about Jesus. Large crowds of people believed his message and got saved. Word of the great outpouring reached Jerusalem, so Peter and John went to see what was happening and to see if they could help. The Bible says the people of Samaria had received Jesus and been baptized in water but they hadn't been baptized in the Holy Spirit. When

they arrived on the scene, Peter and John began to lay hands on the people so they could receive the Holy Spirit.

> Then they laid hands on them, and they received the Holy Spirit. And when Simon saw that through the laying on of the apostles' hands the Holy Spirit was given, he offered them money, saying, "Give me this power also, that anyone on whom I lay hands may receive the Holy Spirit."
>
> Acts 8:17–19 (NKJV)

Simon was amazed at what he saw that day. Judging by his reaction it must have been something similar to the events that took place on the Day of Pentecost. He was a magician in the local area, who believed Philip's message and accepted Jesus. But when he saw what Peter and John were able to do by the laying on of hands, his old show-business mentality came to the surface. Peter rebuffed his offer and told him he couldn't purchase the power of the Holy Spirit with money. What do you think Simon saw that day that got him so excited? I don't think Peter and John prayed with the people and then told them they had now been filled with the Spirit. I believe he saw the fire, he saw the power, and he heard people speaking in tongues. Otherwise why would he want to buy it?

These are the only actual examples we have in the Bible of people being baptized in the Holy Spirit. There are many other references that teach us about the Holy Spirit and speaking in tongues. We'll look at some of those right now. Hopefully you are beginning to see why we Pentecostals believe that the baptism of the Holy Spirit is a distinct event that takes place at some point after we accept Jesus and are born again, and the evidence that we have received it is speaking in tongues.

When we speak in tongues, the Holy Spirit is communicating with our spirit, and we are praying things we do not even understand. God does understand, though, and he is the one giving us the words to say. When we are baptized in the Holy Spirit and begin to speak in tongues, what we are receiving is a personal prayer language. It is a way to communicate with God in a way that is God oriented and not man oriented.

> For he who speaks in a tongue does not speak to men but to God, for no one understands him; however, in the spirit he speaks mysteries.
>
> 1 Corinthians 14:2 (NKJV)

> For if I pray in tongues, my spirit is praying, but I don't understand what I am saying.
>
> 1 Corinthians 14:14 (NLT)

> What is the conclusion then? I will pray with the spirit, and I will also pray with the understanding. I will sing with the spirit, and I will also sing with the understanding.
>
> 1 Corinthians 14:15 (NKJV)

God has given us a great tool to use to help us make it through this life he has given us here on planet Earth. He doesn't want us to just endure and survive; he wants us to flourish and thrive. Who knows more about what we need to do well than God himself? So when we allow him to pray through us, we are praying for things we really need, not what we think we need.

> He who speaks in a tongue edifies himself.
>
> 1 Corinthians 14:4a (NKJV)

The word *edify* means to build up or strengthen. So when we pray in our prayer language, the special language that God gave us, we are building up our strength spiritually. This world we live in will throw a lot of stuff at us to try to tear us down. Satan and his demonic forces will never give up trying to destroy our lives. As a matter of fact, since we have become Christians, they will try even harder. They will do their best to destroy each of us and our families and, if they can, cause us to give up on our Christian life and walk away from it altogether. If Satan and his forces are unsuccessful at that, they will still attempt to cause us so much trouble we will be unable to have any positive impact on the world around us.

> For we are not fighting against flesh-and-blood enemies, but against evil rulers and authorities of the unseen world, against mighty powers in this dark world, and against evil spirits in the heavenly places.
>
> Ephesians 6:12 (NKJV)

> Pray in the Spirit at all times and on every occasion. Stay alert and be persistent in your prayers for all believers everywhere.
>
> Ephesians 6:18 (NLT)

> For the weapons of our warfare are not carnal but mighty in God for pulling down strongholds.
>
> 2 Corinthians 10:4 (NKJV)

These verses talk about a war going on all around us. It is a war for our eternal soul and a war against the souls of all our friends, family, and acquaintances. It is a war against all humankind everywhere. It is a spiritual war that can only be won with spiritual weapons. Remember, Satan is a defeated foe, and he has no real authority in this world. Only through deception and what we allow him does he have any power at all. That word *carnal* in 2 Corinthians 10:4 means earthly or manmade. When we fight against other people and against the difficult situations we face in life with our own human effort, we are using earthly weapons. We cannot win this battle with our earthly weapons. Our enemy is not our spouse, our kids, our employer, the government, the schools, or anything else from our physical world that we feel is rising up against us. It is Satan himself, and he can only be defeated spiritually.

When we get away by ourselves and pray in our prayer language, we are building ourselves up to win that spiritual fight we are in. We can do it anywhere, anytime. In our bedroom, in our kitchen, in our car, at work, or at school.

You might be wondering, *How do I get this amazing gift?* It's easy; ask God for it. He told us over and over in his Word that he will give us whatever we ask for.

> Ask, and it will be given to you; seek, and you will find; knock, and it will be opened to you. For everyone who asks receives, and he who seeks

> finds, and to him who knocks it will be opened. Or what man is there among you who, if his son asks for bread, will give him a stone? Or if he asks for a fish, will he give him a serpent? If you then, being evil, know how to give good gifts to your children, how much more will your Father who is in heaven give good things to those who ask Him!
>
> Matthew 7:7–11 (NKJV)

God sent this special gift just for us, and he will surely give it to you if you ask for it. Earlier we read a story from the book of Acts where Peter was preaching to the household of Cornelius and suddenly the Holy Spirit was poured out on all of them. When that happened Peter said, "I see very clearly that God shows no favoritism. In every nation he accepts those who fear him and do what is right" (Act 10:34, NLT).

The baptism of the Holy Spirit is available to all of us. All we have to do is ask God for it. There is a step of faith involved, and that is just opening our mouths and beginning to speak out in another language. People get it in various ways, in various settings, and in various circumstances. Probably the most common way is in a church service where someone lays hands on you and prays as we read about earlier with Peter, John, Ananias, and Paul. You could be alone praying or in a small group at someone's home. A friend of mine was up late one night walking around his house with his crying baby, and he suddenly started speaking in tongues walking down his hallway. Just ask God right now and trust him to give it to you.

After you receive it, you will have access to your

prayer language whenever you want to use it. It is available twenty-four hours a day, seven days a week. It is not an emotional experience, as some would claim. As a matter of fact, most times no feelings are involved with it at all. But you and God are communicating on a level you can't possibly comprehend. He is building up your spirit to have the strength not only to survive in this world but to flourish.

The Gifts of the Spirit

When you have been baptized in the Holy Spirit, you have access to something else God has given to us while we are here on earth. These are special gifts for us to use in ministering, or serving others.

> There are diversities of gifts, but the same Spirit. There are differences of ministries, but the same Lord. And there are diversities of activities, but it is the same God who works all in all. But the manifestation of the Spirit is given to each one for the profit of all: for to one is given the Word of Wisdom through the Spirit, to another the Word of Knowledge through the same Spirit, to another Faith by the same Spirit, to another Gifts of Healings by the same Spirit, to another the Working of Miracles, to another Prophecy, to another Discerning of Spirits, to another Different Kinds of Tongues, to another the Interpretation of Tongues. But one and the same Spirit works all these things, distributing to each one individually as He wills.
>
> 1 Corinthians 12:4–11 (NKJV)

As a Spirit-filled believer, you have access to each of these gifts to use in service to others. It will depend on the circumstances and the leading of the Holy Spirit which one you need to use to meet the need. Each of them are beyond what we could do in our own natural abilities, so they are supernatural. Let's go through each of them to get an idea what they are all about.

1. *Word of Wisdom.* This is speaking a special word from God into the lives of others. It could involve a decision they need to make or a direction or choice they need to make in life. It might be giving them some advice or instruction on managing their lives successfully. Whatever it is, it will be something you wouldn't have thought of on your own, and it will be the exact answer to their situation.
2. *Word of Knowledge.* This is knowing facts or details about someone or about their life that hasn't been told to you. It was revealed by God. It could be about a past relationship or event that has affected them. It could be something they know about, or it might be something they are unaware of. Most often it will be a way to get to the root of a problem so it can be acknowledged and dealt with. There are times when it might be something you don't even share with the person; it could be something you just pray about.
3. *Faith.* Our Christianity would not be possible without faith. We need it to believe and receive

what Jesus did for us and to trust that everything God has promised us and told us about in his word is true. Hebrews 11:6 tells us, "Without faith it is impossible to please Him" (NKJV). The gift of faith, though, goes even beyond that faith. It comes when you are praying about a particular person or event, when suddenly you know deep down inside of you that God is going to answer your prayer. The circumstances haven't changed; there is nothing outwardly that says anything is going to happen, but the Holy Spirit touched your spirit, and you know beyond the shadow of doubt that the answer is coming.

4. *Gifts of Healings.* As Christians we all have the ability to pray and believe for healing for ourselves and others. But laying hands on the sick and injured and through the power of the Holy Spirit and in the name of Jesus, speaking healing into their lives is the gift of healing. It is especially common for evangelists to use this gift to attract attention to the gospel and bring souls into the kingdom. There have been cases of charlatans and con artists pretending to use this gift in an attempt to gain riches and notoriety. Hollywood and the media will try to tell you it is all a bunch of fakery, but it is really a gift of the Holy Spirit. God will use people to pray for others and touch their lives and bring healing to their physical bodies.

5. *Working of Miracles.* These are any other miracles that take place besides healing for our physical bodies. We pray in the name of Jesus and through

the power of the Holy Spirit see miracles takes place. A miracle is something that goes against the ways of nature and the laws of physics.

6. *Prophecy.* In the same way the Holy Spirit gives us the words to say when we speak in tongues, he gives the words to say when we prophesy. This time though the words are in our own language. This will happen in a gathering of believers, like a church service or a Bible study. Just as tongues are meant to strengthen and build up the individual believer, prophecy is meant to build up and strengthen the entire body of believers.

> But he who prophesies speaks edification and exhortation and comfort to men. He who speaks in a tongue edifies himself, but he who prophesies edifies the church.
>
> 1 Corinthians 14:3–4 (NKJV)

At some point in the meeting of believers, one of the people there who is open to the leading of the Holy Spirit will speak out the very thoughts of God himself. They will be words of encouragement, words of instruction, and possibly words of conviction but never words of condemnation.

> But if all prophesy, and an unbeliever or an uninformed person comes in, he is convinced by all, he is convicted by all. And thus the secrets of his heart are revealed; and so, falling down on his face, he will worship God and report that God is truly among you.
>
> 1 Corinthians 14:24–25 (NKJV)

Notice he says if all prophesy. This is not something for just a few selected people to do, Paul says every one of us should desire to prophesy.

> Pursue love, and desire spiritual gifts, but especially that you may prophesy.
>
> 1 Corinthians 14:1 (NKJV)

7. *Discerning of Spirits.* This is the ability to read and understand the different situations we might find ourselves in as believers and know if there is a good or bad spirit involved. There are times we can walk into a room and just know without anything being said that evil is present. Sometimes people can sound really good and with their words can make us believe just about anything, but a spirit of discernment will let us know that the person has dishonest intentions.

8–9. *Different Kinds of Tongues and Interpretation of Tongues.* I put these two together because they go together and shouldn't be separated. Different kinds of tongues in this case are different than the tongues you received as your prayer language. Here it is something that is done in a public setting just like prophecy. At some point in the meeting, a person will speak out in another language; then the same person or another person present at the meeting will speak out an interpretation.

> I wish you all spoke with tongues, but even more that you prophesied; for he who prophesies is greater than he who speaks with tongues, unless indeed he interprets, that the church may receive edification.
>
> 1 Corinthian 14:5 (NKJV)

So tongues combined with the interpretation in a meeting of believers accomplishes the same thing as prophecy; it edifies the believers. But tongues spoken out in a service have to be interpreted.

> Therefore let him who speaks in a tongue pray that he may interpret. If there is no interpreter, let him keep silent in church, and let him speak to himself and to God. If the whole church comes together in one place, and all speak with tongues, and there come in those who are uninformed or unbelievers, will they not say that you are out of your mind?
>
> 1 Corinthians 14:13, 28, 23 (NKJV)

God gave us all of these special gifts to be used by the believers to minister to people, to impact their lives, and to bring them into a relationship with God. To some it sounds like chaos and confusion, and they will tell you that it must not be from God.

> For God is not the author of confusion but of peace, as in all the churches of the saints.
>
> 1 Corinthians 14:33 (NKJV)

They like that verse, but they forget about the verses right ahead of it.

> Let all things be done for edification. If anyone speaks in a tongue, let there be two or at the most three, each in turn, and let one interpret. But if there

> is no interpreter, let him keep silent in church, and let him speak to himself and to God. Let two or three prophets speak, and let the others judge. But if anything is revealed to another who sits by, let the first keep silent. For you can all prophesy one by one, that all may learn and all may be encouraged. And the spirits of the prophets are subject to the prophets. For God is not the author of confusion but of peace, as in all the churches of the saints.
>
> 1 Corinthians 14:26–33 (NKJV)

Or the verses that come after.

> Therefore, brethren, desire earnestly to prophesy, and do not forbid to speak with tongues. Let all things be done decently and in order.
>
> 1 Corinthians 14:39–40 (NKJV)

God does not demand silence in the church; he demands order. And he thinks we can have order and still include tongues, interpretation, and prophecy. He also thinks we can include words of knowledge, words of wisdom, healing, miracles, faith, and discerning of spirits. Our church services should be exciting and powerful, and we should allow God to truly move and impact the lives of people the way he thinks they need to be touched. When we arrange and organize things to such a point that we don't allow room for God to step in and work on people the way he sees fit, we are suppressing his leading and limiting what he can do.

Conclusion

Learning to listen to the voice of the Holy Spirit and then being willing to follow his guidance as he provides it is a significant step in the life of any believer. Notice I said learning to listen. It is something that has to be learned because we do not come by it naturally. It's like an old-fashioned radio where you had to adjust the knob until you were able to eliminate the noise and static and hear the radio station clearly. We have never been tuned to the frequency of the Holy Spirit's voice, so we need to learn to recognize the sound of his voice. It won't be easy to hear at first because his voice is not very loud.

> "Go out and stand before me on the mountain," the LORD told him. And as Elijah stood there, the LORD passed by, and a mighty windstorm hit the mountain. It was such a terrible blast that the rocks were torn loose, but the LORD was not in the wind. After the wind there was an earthquake, but the LORD was not in the earthquake. [12]And after the earthquake there was a fire, but the LORD was not in the fire. And after the fire there was the sound of a gentle whisper."
>
> 1 Kings 19:11–12 (NLT)

That is how the Holy Spirit will normally speak to us, "a gentle whisper." We live in a hustle-bustle world that is full of noise and distractions. We are on the go all of the time just dealing with the business of life, and we have very little time left simply to settle down and relax. To hear the Holy Spirit, though, we need to stop and listen. We need to turn off the iPod, turn off the TV, turn off the radio, turn off the CD player, and get away from the computer. I know that sounds harsh in this day and age, but you will probably not hear his voice if you don't stop and be quiet.

There are three possible sources of the voices inside of you: your own voice, the voice of evil (Satan or any of his demonic forces), or the voice of the Holy Spirit. Your own voice tends to be self-centered and concerned with your own comfort and survival. Your motivations will be defined by fear and pride. Your own voice will try to keep you out of embarrassing and uncomfortable situations and want to put you in places where you get praise and recognition.

The voice of evil will speak to you of doing wrong. It will try to persuade you to do things that violate your own sense of conscience and morality, but it will make it sound so attractive you will fall for it almost every time. As a matter of fact, since your own sinful nature has such an inclination toward evil, you will almost be powerless to stop yourself from getting involved. After he has you hooked, Satan switches to a new ploy and attacks you with guilt and condemnation. He will tell you what a horrible person you are and how you are obviously a hopeless cause. He will make you question your faith and make you wonder how you ever thought it would be possible for you to really change.

When the Holy Spirit speaks to you in that small, quiet voice, he will always lead you to do good. He will talk to you of serving others and not yourself. His voice won't be that hard to recognize; you just have to get used to it. He will help you overcome the schemes of the enemy if you are willing to listen and head in the other direction when you are tempted. When you mess up, the Holy Spirit will bring conviction to your heart rather than condemnation, as Satan does. The difference is that conviction doesn't accuse you of being rotten; it lets you know you are still loved and that there is a better way if you learn to make better choices.

This brings us to the second part of being led by the Holy Spirit, obeying what he directs you to do. This is kind of like when you join the gym because you want to get stronger and get in shape. You start with the small weights, and over time you begin to build the amount of weight you are lifting, and you start to see some results in your body. When we are being led by the Holy Spirit, we start with small steps, and each time we hear his voice and are obedient to his leading, we get a little stronger. Eventually we will get to the point we can hear his voice anytime and anywhere. It is still important for us to take that quiet time every day to listen and spend time with him, but once we are familiar with his voice, we could recognize it in the middle of downtown traffic or sitting in an NFL stadium full of screaming fans.

Sometimes the Holy Spirit will challenge you to step out and do something you are not necessarily comfortable with. It will go against your own sense of comfort and self-respect, but when you step out, you will be expanding your territory and accomplishing things you never thought you could.

Listening to and obeying the Holy Spirit is what determines how far you advance in your Christian walk. The more you listen and the more you obey, the more stable and blessed your own life becomes and the more impact you have on the world around you.

A New Way of Thinking

> "Don't copy the behavior and customs of this world, but let God transform you into a new person by changing the way you think. Then you will know what God wants you to do, and you will know how good, and pleasing, and perfect his will really is."
>
> Romans 12:2 (NLT)

Principle 7 – As Christians we believe that for us to truly discover the purpose and destiny God created us for we will have to allow God to change the way we think.

I am extremely excited to write this chapter of my book. Everything I have written up until now has just been building to this point. As I mentioned to you earlier, I grew up in church. I got saved when I was a little boy and got baptized in the Holy Spirit when I was a teenager. I have been taught most of the information I have been sharing with you in this book over the course of my entire life. I always felt a sense of disconnect, though, between all of these Bible truths and real life. It wasn't that I was living a wicked or rebellious life or anything like that; it was just that I didn't feel as though I were living the victorious and abundant life I knew the Scriptures promised me. I kind of felt helpless and a little bit hypocritical because I didn't understand how to make all of this Bible stuff really apply to my life.

What I didn't realize, and as far as I can remember had never been taught, was that my thinking needed to change. I have mentioned in earlier chapters that we have developed a certain way of thinking and responding to life, based on how we were raised, what we have been taught, and the events and circumstances of our lives. Unfortunately for most of us, what we've learned through our many life experiences is called "stinkin' thinkin'." We have a very limited and negative view of life, possibilities, and potential. We tend to think of life in terms of the haves and the have-nots. We think some people have special abilities, some are born with a silver spoon and get all the breaks, others just happen to be in the right place at the right time, while the rest of us are just destined to barely get by. Life is just too hard, and our circumstances seem too difficult to overcome; so we assume we just weren't meant to accomplish much with our lives. Oh sure, we might be able to get a job and maybe put together a decent life, but the great things in life will be achieved by others.

What we fail to understand is that God has destined us all for greatness. He has put the potential inside each of us to accomplish amazing and wonderful things. In Romans 12:2 above, we are told that if we are to know what God wants us to do and how good, and pleasing, and perfect his will really is, we are going to have to let him change the way we think.

I think this is why so many of us Christians struggle in our daily walk. Even though we have accepted Jesus, our sins are forgiven, our spirits have been regenerated, and we have the Holy Spirit available to help us and guide us through life, we have never learned to stop thinking the way the world thinks. And what we really don't understand is that in order to stop thinking the way world thinks, we need to start thinking the way God thinks.

That verse begins by saying, "Don't copy the behavior and customs of this world." As Christians we need to learn not to think about things the way the world thinks about them, the way it thinks about marriage, parenting, finances, working, playing, anything. It is the way we have been taught to think and the way we have learned to act, but it is totally off base and counter to God's thinking and God's way of doing things.

The next part of the verse says, "but let God transform you into a new person." The Greek word here that is translated *transform* is *metamorpho.* It is where we get the English word *metamorphosis.* Back in high school, we learned in our science classes that this is what a tadpole does when it turns into a frog and what a caterpillar does when it turns into a butterfly. If you like science fiction and comic books, you might remember it is what Dr. Bruce Banner went through when he turned into the Incredible Hulk. It means to change completely from one form to another. In other words, instead of thinking like the world, we have to completely change and learn to think as God thinks.

Then this verse tells how God is going to change us. It says, "by changing the way you think." It's easy to say we need to change but another thing altogether to explain how to bring about that change. This is the area of this teaching that went beyond anything I had ever heard before. What I had to realize is how my way of thinking had brought me to the point my life was at that moment and then how to make changes in my thinking to bring about the things God really wanted to accomplish with my life.

Remember back in chapter three where we talked about our souls being the way we think, the way we feel, the way we respond to different situations, and the way we make decisions? Then in chapter five we learned that this whole changing-how-we-think process takes place in our soul. Our spirit was born again the minute we accepted Jesus, but now our soul needs to change. It doesn't happen overnight; it is a process we commit to that will last a lifetime. You can be stubborn and stay the way you are right now, but wouldn't you rather see what God really has for you? Changing how you think is really a commitment to change. Have you ever tried to not think about something? It's pretty much impossible, isn't it? So you can't just stop thinking as the world thinks; you have to learn to think the way God thinks, the way he thinks about marriage, parenting, finances, working, playing, everything. When we do that, the ways of this world will eventually just fall away. We talked about the Holy Spirit working on us and challenging us to change. He will convict us, teach us, and lead us into change if we let him.

Some Truths about Ourselves

We will never be able to change if we don't come to some realizations of how we got to where we are right now and what it will take to bring about the changes we need to make.

1. *You are where you are right now because of the choices you've made in the past.* As human beings we like to blame others for our problems. It really makes us feel better if we can find somebody else to hold responsible for the mess we're in. It's the schools, the government, my parents, my wife, my boss; it has got to be somebody's fault life turned out this way. It started way back in the Garden of Eden when God confronted the first man and woman for their sin. Adam blamed his wife; then he blamed God for giving him his wife, and Eve blamed the serpent.

We all have bad things happen to us, and some of us have had some really terrible things happen to us. It's not the circumstances themselves, though, that determine where our lives go; it is how we respond to them and the attitude we have as we are going through them that makes the difference. We all know of people who have gone through some horrific event or circumstance but then have made it through the ordeal successfully and come out on the other side as winners. We also know people who have had some difficult or terrible thing happen in their lives, and they never bounce back from it. It destroys their life and their relationships and sends them down a road that they never totally recover from.

Our own choices, or lack thereof, will determine where our life goes.

> Do not be deceived, God is not mocked; for whatever a man sows, that he will also reap.
>
> Galatians 6:7 (NKJV)

We like to say that life is not fair, and to a certain extent that's true, but in this way it is absolutely fair. We will all reap the harvest of our own choices. If we make good choices, we will reap good results, and if we make bad choices, we will reap bad results. The unfair part is there might be others in our lives that will also reap some bad results from our bad choices. And of course there are also people in our lives that will make bad choices and cause us to reap difficult times. But remember, it is our own attitude and how we respond that will ultimately determine how well our life goes.

2. *Your responses are preprogrammed.* It's what's inside of us that determines what comes out when the pressure's on. We are like a computer; whatever is programmed inside of us is what comes out. We can all sound and look good in church on Sunday morning when we are trying to put on a good show, but what comes out of our mouth and what do we do when things are not going our way?

> Either make the tree good and its fruit good, or else make the tree bad and its fruit bad; for a tree

> is known by its fruit. Brood of vipers! How can you, being evil, speak good things? For out of the abundance of the heart the mouth speaks. A good man out of the good treasure of his heart brings forth good things, and an evil man out of the evil treasure brings forth evil things.
>
> Matthew 12:33–35 (NKJV)

> For as he thinks in his heart, so is he.
>
> Proverbs 23:7 (NKJV)

If what we have inside of us is good, then good things come out when the pressure is on. When we find ourselves under pressure and things are not going our way, if bad language, anger, or depression are what come out, then we know what has been programmed inside of us.

3. *You can change what's inside of you and change how you respond to circumstances.* Notice in that verse above where Jesus said, "make the tree good and its fruit will be good." We tend to think that we are stuck being the way we are just because that's how we are. We think we have an "Irish temper," or my daddy was an alcoholic so I am too, or I was abused as a child so I can't help it when I'm angry or when I abuse my children too.

This might be a new concept for many of you, but we are not stuck being as we are just because that's how we are. We can make the choice to change.

Albert Einstein put it this way: "*Insanity is doing the same thing over and over and expecting to get different results.*"[6]

We cannot keep acting the same way we have always acted and expect our lives to change. It just doesn't work that way. If we truly want to change, we are going to have to make some different choices.

Here is a little saying for you to learn: if you want something you've never had before, you'll have to do something you've never done before.

So much of our lives we just try to get by and spend our time wishing and hoping life will get better. But we need to rise up and take control of our own lives. We have got to quit wishing, and we have to quit blaming. We are going to have to take some positive, proactive steps to truly change our lives. We need to change what is on the inside of us so we can change what comes out. To change truly we need to replace our old rotten way of thinking with God's amazing way of thinking.

What Are God's Thoughts?

We have a lot of confusion and wrong ideas about God and his plans. The first thing we need to change is our perception of God and how he thinks about us.

> "For I know the thoughts that I think toward you," says the LORD, "thoughts of peace and not of evil, to give you a future and a hope."
>
> Jeremiah 29:11 (NKJV)

That is how God thinks about you. He has great plans for you; he wants to give you a future and a hope. Never believe the lies of the enemy. No matter how bleak the circumstances, there is always a hope and a future. There is a story in the Bible about a man named Job. He went through some devastating circumstances, and his life and his future looked hopeless. But he never gave up on God, and God never gave up on him. It is estimated that his difficult time lasted between eleven and thirteen months; then God restored everything back to him and more. He had been a very blessed man before the terrible ordeal he went through, but the Bible says he was even more blessed in the latter part of his life than he was in the first. He went on to lead a very long and fulfilling life.

God desires for you to live an abundant and blessed life.

I am not sure where the belief came from that says that being poor is more righteous than being rich. I can assure you of this much: it is not the Bible! God does not want us to be poor, and he does not want us to take a vow of poverty. If God wanted us poor, then there would not be so many promises of blessing in his word. God loves it when we do well. He wants to see us prosper and be blessed in our finances, in our marriages, with our children, at the job, and at school. Wherever and whatever we do, God wants to see us do well and have success.

> Let the LORD be magnified, Who has pleasure in the prosperity of His servant.
>
> Psalm 35:27 (NKJV)

> Jesus said, "I have come that they may have life, and that they may have it more abundantly."
>
> John 10:10 (NKJV)

God takes pleasure in you doing well and he sent his Son so you can do just that, do well. He wants you to have an abundant life. He only gives us one stipulation to receiving his blessing in our lives; we have to be obedient to his Word.

> If you are willing and obedient, you shall eat the good of the land.
>
> Isaiah 1:19 (NKJV)

When we are obedient to God's Word and willingly submit to his authority in our lives, the promises he lays out before us are pretty incredible.

> If you fully obey the LORD your God and carefully keep all his commands that I am giving you today, the LORD your God will set you high above all the nations of the world. You will experience all these blessings if you obey the LORD your God: Your towns and your fields will be blessed. Your children and your crops will be blessed. The offspring of your herds and flocks will be blessed. Your fruit baskets and breadboards will be blessed. Wherever you go and whatever you do, you will be blessed. The LORD will conquer your enemies when they attack you. They will attack you from one direction, but they will scatter from you in seven! The LORD will guarantee a blessing on everything you do and will fill your storehouses with grain. The LORD your God will bless you in the land he is giving you. If you obey the commands of the LORD your

> God and walk in his ways, the LORD will establish you as his holy people as he swore he would do. Then all the nations of the world will see that you are a people claimed by the Lord, and they will stand in awe of you. The LORD will give you prosperity in the land he swore to your ancestors to give you, blessing you with many children, numerous livestock, and abundant crops. The LORD will send rain at the proper time from his rich treasury in the heavens and will bless all the work you do. You will lend to many nations, but you will never need to borrow from them. If you listen to these commands of the LORD your God that I am giving you today, and if you carefully obey them, the LORD will make you the head and not the tail, and you will always be on top and never at the bottom.
>
> Deuteronomy 28:1–13 (NLT)

This is an amazing passage of Scripture recording the words of Moses to the people of Israel of God's plans for them if they lived in obedience to the commands and requirements of God. Those same promises hold true for all of us when we choose to live in obedience to his leading. In the last chapter we talked about living a Holy Spirit-led life and how important that is to our Christian growth. Remember I said the Holy Spirit will never force himself on us; we still have the choice to listen or not listen, to live in obedience or to live in rebellion.

> Now listen! Today I am giving you a choice between life and death, between prosperity and disaster. For I command you this day to love the LORD your God and to keep his commands,

> decrees, and regulations by walking in his ways. Today I have given you the choice between life and death, between blessings and curses. Now I call on heaven and earth to witness the choice you make. Oh, that you would choose life, so that you and your descendants might live! You can make this choice by loving the LORD your God, obeying him, and committing yourself firmly to him. This is the key to your life.
>
> Deuteronomy 30:15–16, 19–20 (NLT)

If you make the choice to obey God's direction for your life, you are going to live under the blessing. The reason God is going to bless you is because he wants to use you.

> Always remember that it is the LORD your God who gives you power to become rich, and he does it to fulfill the covenant he made with your ancestors.
>
> Deuteronomy 8:18 (NLT)

God's covenant that he made is the good news that Jesus Christ came and shed his blood, gave his life, and restored all of us back to himself.

> The Lord isn't really being slow about his promise, as some people think. No, he is being patient for your sake. He does not want anyone to be destroyed, but wants everyone to repent.
>
> 2 Peter 3:9 (NLT)

God wants everyone in the world to get saved, but to do that he needs you. If you are caught up in your own struggles and barely getting by yourself, how effective are you going to be in reaching a lost and dying world?

God has a plan and a destiny for your life.

There is a reason God put you in this place, at this time. He could have put you anywhere in the world at any time in history, but he chose right here and right now.

> For we are His workmanship, created in Christ Jesus for good works, which God prepared beforehand that we should walk in them.
>
> Ephesians 2:10 (NKJV)

You were not an accident. God chose you before the very foundation of the world. It doesn't matter what your parents were thinking; God had a plan.

Have you ever heard someone say, "I don't need to be rich, all I need is enough to get by, enough to live in a decent house, drive a decent car, and pay my bills." Maybe you've thought that yourself. It sounds quite humble, even noble, but it is also selfish and unbiblical. God has plans for us, and they involve impacting the lives of others, not just living for ourselves.

> And God will generously provide all you need. Then you will always have everything you need and plenty left over to share with others.
>
> 2 Corinthians 9:8 (NLT)

See, we can have enough to live in a decent house, drive a decent car, and pay our bills, but then have so much left over that it is available for every good work that comes our way. God wants to reach the world, and he needs you to do it.

God has a purpose for each of us and a great plan to fulfill that purpose. You were destined for greatness, and you will never find true happiness and fulfillment until you discover what that destiny is. If you live for yourself, you will never find it.

> For whoever desires to save his life will lose it, but whoever loses his life for My sake will find it.
>
> Matthew 16:25 (NKJV)

Satan is determined to destroy God's plan.

Satan is resolute in his determination to make sure that we never fulfill God's purpose for our lives. He will do everything within his power to destroy us. He will steal from us, and if he can, he will kill us.

> The thief's [Satan's] purpose is to steal and kill and destroy.
>
> John 10:10 (NLT)

He wants to use us as doormats. He wants to use us as punching bags. He wants to keep us down and out. He wants to keep us sick and tired. As long as we let him get away with it, he will continue to torment us. When we get to the point we are sick and tired of being sick and tired, we can put a stop to it.

> You are of God, little children, and have overcome them, because He who is in you is greater than he who is in the world.
>
> 1 John 4:4 (NKJV)

When we are born again and we have the Holy Spirit residing inside of us, Satan and his demonic forces have no power over us unless we allow it.

Remember, in the spiritual world, we are sitting right there with Jesus at the right hand of the Father, and all principalities and powers in this world are under our feet.

> This is the same mighty power that raised Christ from the dead and seated him in the place of honor at God's right hand in the heavenly realms. Now he is far above any ruler or authority or power or leader or anything else—not only in this world but also in the world to come. God has put all things under the authority of Christ and has made him head over all things for the benefit of the church.
>
> Ephesians 1:20–22 (NLT)

> For he raised us from the dead along with Christ and seated us with him in the heavenly realms because we are united with Christ Jesus.
>
> Ephesians 2:6 (NLT)

God put everything in this world under our feet and gave us authority over all of them. Now all we need to do is speak to them in the name of Jesus and command them to leave us alone. Here is what you say, "Satan, I have been bought with the blood of Jesus, and you have no business in my life. I take my authority over you and command you to leave in the name of Jesus!" He has to leave; he has no choice. He must always submit to the name of Jesus. Remember, he is a defeated foe.

Did you know that, as a believer, God has built a huge barrier around you? The Bible calls it a hedge of protection. Satan cannot even get to you unless he asks permission. We learned earlier that Satan wanders the earth looking for someone to destroy.

> Stay alert! Watch out for your great enemy, the devil. He prowls around like a roaring lion, looking for someone to devour.
>
> 1 Peter 5:8 (NLT)

When he sees us with that giant hedge God built all around us, he doesn't even bother. He knows there is nothing he can do. There are times though when God might allow Satan to have access to us if he has something he wants to develop in our life. We have an example of this in the book of Job.

> Now there was a day when the sons of God came to present themselves before the LORD, and Satan also came among them. And the LORD said to Satan, "From where do you come?"
>
> So Satan answered the LORD and said, "From going to and fro on the earth, and from walking back and forth on it."
>
> Then the LORD said to Satan, "Have you considered My servant Job, that there is none like him on the earth, a blameless and upright man, one who fears God and shuns evil?"
>
> So Satan answered the LORD and said, "Does Job fear God for nothing? Have You not made a hedge around him, around his household, and around all that he has on every side? You have blessed the work of his hands, and his possessions have increased in the land. But now, stretch out Your hand and touch all that he has, and he will surely curse You to Your face!"

> And the Lord said to Satan, "Behold, all that he has is in your power; only do not lay a hand on his person."
>
> Job 1:6–12 (NLT)

Here we see a real-life example of Satan wandering the earth and the hedge God has built around his followers. Notice Satan didn't have access to Job until God gave it to him. Also notice that God never did anything to Job, but for some reason he allowed Satan to cause devastation in Job's life.

As was mentioned earlier, Job did go through a very difficult time in his life; but God helped him through it, and he came out on the other side even more blessed than he was before.

Then, in the book of Luke, Jesus tells Peter that Satan has asked for him.

> And the Lord said, "Simon, Simon! Indeed, Satan has asked for you, that he may sift you as wheat. But I have prayed for you, that your faith should not fail; and when you have returned to Me, strengthen your brethren."
>
> Luke 22:31–32 (NKJV)

Simon is his real name; Jesus called him Peter, which means *rock.* God was planning on using Peter to help build the foundation of his church. Satan asked for access to Peter because he wanted to destroy him. God had big plans for Peter, so he was not going to let Satan defeat him. He did give Satan access to him, however, because he knew that Satan's attack would strengthen Peter. Because of what he went through,

Peter became extremely strong in his faith and was indeed one of the founding fathers of the Christian church. What Satan meant for evil, God used for good.

> And we know that all things work together for good to those who love God, to those who are the called according to His purpose.
>
> Romans 8:28 (NKJV)

Satan will ask for permission to destroy each of us because he wants to do just that, destroy us. God has big plans for us though, so he will not allow Satan to defeat us. If God feels there is something we need to learn, he might allow Satan access for a short time, but he will walk right through the time of difficulty with us and bring us out on the other side victorious.

Sometimes, because even as Christians we still have a sinful and fallen nature, we get involved with things we shouldn't and allow things in our lives that are not supposed to be there. When we do that, we will cause some gaps to develop in our hedges. Then when Satan sees us, as he is wandering to and fro looking for someone to destroy, he can get right through our hedge and cause trouble in our lives without even asking God for permission. Since we still belong to God and are called according to his purpose, God will still cause good to come from our times of trouble because he is faithful to his word. But it was a test we didn't have to go through that we brought on ourselves because of our own foolishness.

Those who are not born again have no hedge of protection around them at all and are wide open to

Satan's destructive schemes. He is free to do whatever he wants in their lives with no restrictions. And we know what he wants; he wants to kill, steal, and destroy. We see plenty of evidence of that every night when we watch the news. God is faithful, and he will still bring good into people's lives from their times of difficulty, despite the fact they will still have nothing to do with him.

How Do We Apply God's Plan?

In order to make God's thought's our thoughts, we need to put God's Word inside of us. Then we have to let God's words be what comes out of us. To put God's thoughts inside of us, we will have to read, study, and memorize God's Word. Then we need to develop the habit of praying and speaking God's words in every situation we might face in life. That doesn't mean we have to become some kind of religious fruitcake. It just means that when issues come up, instead of the negative words we normally respond with, we learn to respond with God's words.

Put God's Word inside of you.

This is a commitment we all need to make. We need to develop the habit of spending time every day reading and studying our Bibles. At first it will seem difficult and confusing, but as you get used to it, you will begin to pick up things and gain understanding that you can apply to your life. You don't have to commit hours to it, although it would have a huge impact on you if you did. For most of us, it is quite difficult to add reading our Bibles to our already busy schedules. Just a few minutes a day is all it takes; fifteen to thirty minutes every day will change your life if you are willing to commit to it.

One thing you can do to help with your understanding is choose an easy-to-read version of the Bible. I would recommend the New Living Translation, the New International Version, or the New King James Version. And get one with some good editor's notes to help explain things to you as you are reading. I like the Spirit-Filled Life Bible and the Life Application Bible. There are many others to choose from, and they can all add some new insight and understanding to your life. A paraphrase version like the Living Bible or the Message Bible will also improve your understanding.

Another step we can take to put God's thoughts inside of us is to memorize. I know this sounds difficult, especially as we get older. But it actually is not as hard as we think. Choose verses that have a particular application to your life and put them in your heart so you can use them every day.

> I have hidden your word in my heart, that I might not sin against you.
>
> Psalm 119:11 (NLT)

A good verse to start with is Jeremiah 29:11. It was just mentioned earlier in this chapter. It is a good verse to keep inside of us, that the God of this universe is actually thinking about you and that he has great plans for you. So start with the first part of the verse, "For I know the thoughts that I think toward you," says the LORD. Repeat that over and over until you have it down. Then move on to the next section, "thoughts of peace and not of evil." Repeat that until you have it down and then combine both parts and repeat them together. Once you have that down move on to the last part of the verse, "to give you a future and a hope" (Jeremiah 29:11). Do the same as before, repeat that until you have it down, and then combine it with the rest of the verse until you can say the whole thing. Don't forget to add the reference with it as you quote it, "Jeremiah 29:11." It will help you with your understanding of the Bible if you know where to find the verses you memorize.

You can memorize from any of the versions you want to. Most of the verses I know are from New King James Version, but you can use any of them.

Once you have that first one down, pick another. "I can do all things through Christ who strengthens me" (Philippians 4:13, NKJV*)* is a good one. Then you can quote it whenever a difficult situation or a challenge comes up in your life.

Here is a list of powerful verses you can memorize. When you have these verses down, don't stop there; the list is endless. Once you get God's Word inside of you, you'll put your enemy on the run, and he will lose.

Deuteronomy 8:18	Joshua 1:8	Psalm 35:27
Matthew 6:33	Matthew 7:7	Matthew 11:28
Matthew 28:19	John 3:16	John 10:10
John 14:6	John 14:12–14	Acts 1:8
Romans 6:23	Romans 8:11	Romans 10:9–10
Romans 12:2	Corinthians 5:17	Galatians 5:22–23
Ephesians 2:5	Ephesians 2:8–10	Ephesians 6:12
Philippians 1:6	Philippians 4:8	2 Thessalonians 3:3
2 Timothy 3:16	Hebrews 4:12	1 John 5:14–15

Learn to speak and pray the Word of God.

Once you begin to put God's Word in your heart, develop the habit of speaking it out loud. Instead of the negative words of defeat we've learned to say whenever we face adversity, we can learn to speak the Word of God.

When we face sickness, we can say, "By his stripes I am healed" (Isaiah 53:5, NKJV).

When we face financial pressures, we can say, "My God will take care of all of my needs according to his riches in glory" (Philippians 4:19, NKJV).

When we face any difficult situation, we can say, "I can do all things through Christ who strengthens me" (Philippians 4:13, NKJV).

Set the priorities of your life to match God's priorities.

This is part of changing the way we think by learning to think the way God thinks. Most of us just kind of drift through life without ever making a conscious decision to set our priorities; they just kind of set themselves. Our priorities are wrapped up in ourselves. We are self-centered, and the most important thing to us is whatever we have determined will make us happy or bring us pleasure at the moment. It might be work, money, entertainment, sports, or family; they all bring pleasure and can be fun. The reality, though, is we will never truly find pleasure or happiness until we learn to line our priorities up with God's priorities. When we do that, we will find that we have time for all of those things. None of them in themselves is bad. As a matter of fact, they are all good, and some are very important. It's just that if any of them are at the top of our priority list our lives are out of order.

The two fundamental elements of our lives that reveal our priorities are our time and our money. Whatever is most important in our lives is what we will spend our money on and what we will spend our time doing. If your life seems too hectic and out of control and your money seems to disappear before your eyes, your priorities are probably mixed up.

As I take you through God's priority list for you, I will try to show you how that affects both your time and your money.

1. Your relationship with God.

This has been the central theme of this book. We were created to have a relationship with God. For human beings, that relationship was destroyed and God stepped in to restore it. Now that we are back in relationship with God, we have to make that relationship our top priority. God created us, put us on this planet he created for us, and designed an abundant and fulfilling life for each of us. In our limited way of looking at life, we think, *If I make God the center of my life, it is going to be dull and dreary, I won't have any fun, and I'll be broke all the time.* Actually, the opposite is true. God designed an exciting and fulfilling life for us. If we strive for the pleasure and excitement, we will find it to be fleeting and hard to sustain, but if we center our lives around God, we will find satisfaction and happiness that we never thought possible.

> But seek first the kingdom of God and His righteousness, and all these things shall be added to you.
>
> Matthew 6:33 (NKJV)

God and Your Time–This is a big first step for most new Christians. Many of us who have been saved for a while still have a hard time in this area. Here are the ways you center your time around God:

First, you have to be involved in a local church. Notice I didn't just say attend church. It is important for our growth as Christians to go beyond just attending church and get involved with our church. Many of us struggle with being a part of church. We might have had bad experiences in our past, we might not see the relevance of church, or we might think we just don't have the time for church. Church is God's plan, though; it is where we are going to be taught, where we are going to grow, and where we are going to change. It is where we are going to develop and discover what God's plan and design is for our life. The Bible says that Jesus gave us some special gifts to aid in our development. These gifts are found at church, so if we reject church we are rejecting the gifts that Jesus gave us.

> Now these are the gifts Christ gave to the church: the apostles, the prophets, the evangelists, and the pastors and teachers. Their responsibility is to equip God's people to do his work and build up the church, the body of Christ.
>
> Ephesians 4:11–12 (NLT)

Jesus gave those men and women to us: apostles who establish our churches, evangelists who bring new believers into our churches, prophets who speak the Word of God into our churches, and pastors and teachers who shepherd us, take care of us, and teach us the ways of God and how to apply them to our lives.

Why did he give them to us? So we could be equipped to do God's work and to build up the church. The Greek word that is translated *equip* in our English versions of the Bible has a dual meaning. First it suggests mending and healing. Like when you have a broken bone and it is set so it can mend and heal. When we become a part of a church and come under the teaching and leadership of the men and women of God, they take our broken and messed-up lives, teach us how to put them back together, and put us on track to live healthy and stable lives.

The second part of the word has to do with a discovering of destiny. When we come under the guidance and authority of God's leaders, we will be able to discover what God's plan and design for our lives truly is. Without putting ourselves in a position where these men and women of God can speak into our lives and challenge us to grow, I don't think it would be possible to figure out God's plan and design for us. Keep in mind that each of these leaders has gone through that same process themselves. They have had leaders help them put their lives together and challenge them to change and grow. Otherwise they wouldn't be in the position to speak into our lives.

Another thing we receive by being part of a church is fellowship and encouragement. We live in a world full of negativity and discouragement. When we gather together with our fellow believers, we put ourselves in the position to be strengthened, motivated, and encouraged.

> Let us think of ways to motivate one another to acts of love and good works. And let us not neglect our meeting together, as some people do, but encourage one another, especially now that the day of his return is drawing near.
>
> Hebrews 10:24–25 (NLT)

One more thing we get from being part of a church is faith.

> So then faith comes by hearing, and hearing by the word of God.
>
> Romans 10:17 (NKJV)

Being in church is where you hear the Word of God, and that is where our faith comes from. When we hear the preachers and the teachers, when we sing the songs, and when we hear the testimonies of what God is doing in the lives of others, we are building our faith.

Don't reject this special gift that was given to you by Jesus himself. Get actively involved in your church. Attend as many of the services as you can possibly get to and get involved in a small group if your church has them. It will impact your life in ways you never thought possible.

You also need to spend time with God praying and reading his Word for yourself. We've already talked about this quite a bit; so I won't go into it too much more, but learn to make it a priority to spend at least some time every day praying, reading, studying, and memorizing God's Word. And don't forget to use your prayer language every day. God wants you to live a victorious and abundant life, and these are the tools he has given you to bring it about.

God and Your Money–Our time was the first step; this second step is the biggest challenge. We don't like people messing with our money. The common perception among most people is that the church and church leaders are greedy and all they want is my money. The truth is, that is how God set it up. Every ministry in the kingdom of God is designed to operate on the donations of God's people. When God's people don't give, the ministries don't survive. We do need to be careful and be wise in our giving because there are thieves and frauds in the church world just as there are in every other profession in the world. Despite the popular opinion, though, I don't think the percentage of the greedy and dishonest is any higher in church than it is anywhere else. There are many honest real-estate agents, but the dishonest few give all the others a bad name. There are many honest lawyers, but the dishonest few give all the others a bad name. The same is true of any profession you can think of: doctors, carpenters, policemen, and salesman. And it is the same for preachers. Don't let the dishonest few cloud your view of all of them. Just be wise.

When God commands us to be givers, he is really testing our attitude. If we are tight with our money and refuse to give, we are being selfish and greedy. We are serving money instead of serving God.

> No one can serve two masters. For you will hate one and love the other; you will be devoted to one and despise the other. You cannot serve both God and money.
>
> Luke 16:13 (NLT)

Instead of being selfish with our money, God wants us to be cheerful givers.

> You must each decide in your heart how much to give. And don't give reluctantly or in response to pressure. For God loves a person who gives cheerfully.
>
> 2 Corinthians 9:7 (NLT)

That Greek word that is translated *cheerfully* is *hillaros.* It is where we get our English word *hilarious.* God wants you to be a hilarious giver, someone that is excited to give and always looking for more opportunities to serve, to help, and to give. Giving is the basis of that abundant life we have been talking about. When we are willing to give, then God gives to us.

> Give, and you will receive. Your gift will return to you in full—pressed down, shaken together to make room for more, running over, and poured into your lap. The amount you give will determine the amount you get back.
>
> Luke 6:38 (NLT)

God has a definite plan of how we are to give and an order for our giving. When we follow God's plan, God's blessings will follow us.

1. *The Tithe*–this is the English translation of a Hebrew word that means one-tenth. God wants us to give one-tenth of our income to him as a tithe. This is his plan for operating and supporting his church. A church has to operate as a business, and we know businesses need an income to operate. As with any business, there is an incredible amount of expense just functioning from week to week. They have lease or mortgage payments, salaries, utilities, supplies, and other expenses that never end. I have heard many complain about pastors' salaries, but why shouldn't a person who has devoted his life to study and service be rewarded for his hard work? And if he has special abilities and the anointing of God on his life that causes him to attract more people and have his church's size increase, then why shouldn't he be rewarded even more? Here is how the Apostle Paul put it:

> Elders who do their work well should be respected and paid well, especially those who work hard at both preaching and teaching. For the Scripture says, "You must not muzzle an ox to keep it from eating as it treads out the grain." And in another place, "Those who work deserve their pay!"
>
> 1 Timothy 5:17–18 (NLT)

The practice of giving and tithing goes back to the very beginning when Cain and Able brought offerings to the Lord.

> When they grew up, Abel became a shepherd, while Cain cultivated the ground. When it was time for the harvest, Cain presented some of his crops as a gift to the LORD. Abel also brought a gift—the best of the firstborn lambs from his flock. The LORD accepted Abel and his gift, but he did not accept Cain and his gift. This made Cain very angry, and he looked dejected.
>
> Genesis 4:2–5 (NLT)

The lesson to be learned from this story is that God demands our first and our best, not our leftovers. Later in the book of Genesis, Abram gives a tithe to a priest named Melchizedek.

> And Melchizedek, the king of Salem and a priest of God Most High, brought Abram some bread and wine. Melchizedek blessed Abram with this blessing: "Blessed be Abram by God Most High, Creator of heaven and earth. And blessed be God Most High, who has defeated your enemies for you." Then Abram gave Melchizedek a tenth of all the goods he had recovered.
>
> Genesis 14:18–20 (NLT)

After the nation of Israel was formed, God laid down some definite rules for tithing. He established it as the way to support his work and those who carry it out. In the nation of Israel, there were twelve tribes descended from the sons of Israel (Jacob), the grandson of Abraham. One of the tribes, Levi, was set aside to do the work of the Lord and take care of the tabernacle (God's house). The priests would also come from the tribe of Levi. The other tribes then were assigned to work the land, raise flocks and herds, start their businesses, and then bring in a tithe of their income, which would be used to support the tribe of Levi and the tabernacle.

> Only the Levites may serve at the Tabernacle, and they will be held responsible for any offenses against it. This is a permanent law for you, to be observed from generation to generation. The Levites will receive no allotment of land among the Israelites, because I have given them the Israelites' tithes, which have been presented as sacred offerings to the LORD. This will be the Levites' share. That is why I said they would receive no allotment of land among the Israelites.
>
> Numbers 18:23–24 (NLT)

God has the same plan for taking care of his church today. The Pastor, his associates, and the paid staff manage and attend to the business of running and maintaining the church. The rest of us then are required to go out and work and bring in our tithes so the church can be healthy and function properly. So many churches struggle financially, and it shouldn't be that way. If those of us in the body of Christ would fulfill our responsibility to support our churches, all of the pressure and anxiety our pastors are forced to deal with every day would disappear. If we are part of a church body, we receive the blessings of being connected with that church. We are provided with the teaching, the building and strengthening, the encouragement, and the fellowship that come with being a member of the family. If we receive all of those blessings and then don't tithe and give to the ministries of the church, we are basically freeloading. We are receiving the benefits of being part of a church body and not paying for it. God is not pleased; as a matter of fact, he gets quite angry about it.

> Will a man rob God? Yet you have robbed Me! But you say, "In what way have we robbed You?" In tithes and offerings. You are cursed with a curse, for you have robbed Me.
>
> Malachi 3:8–9 (NKJV)

If we don't pay our tithes, God considers it stealing, and he says we are living under a curse. Here is something else the Bible says about us if we do not take care of his house.

> You have planted much but harvest little. You eat but are not satisfied. You drink but are still thirsty. You put on clothes but cannot keep warm. Your wages disappear as though you were putting them in pockets filled with holes!
>
> Haggai 1:6 (NLT)

If we do pay our tithes though, we are living under blessing.

> "Bring all the tithes into the storehouse so there will be enough food in my Temple. If you do," says the Lord of Heaven's Armies, "I will open the windows of heaven for you. I will pour out a blessing so great you won't have enough room to take it in! Try it! Put me to the test! Your crops will be abundant, for I will guard them from insects and disease. Your grapes will not fall from the vine before they are ripe. Then all nations will call you blessed, for your land will be such a delight."
>
> Malachi 3:10–12 (NLT)

This is the only place in the Bible that God says to test him. This might sound hard to believe, but with God's blessing on your finances because you are a tither, you will live better on the 90 percent you have left over after you pay your tithe than you did with the 100 percent and doing it on your own. This goes against our normal way of thinking: *How can I afford to give God* 10 *percent of my money when I'm already broke and don't have enough to make it from one paycheck to the next?* This is why God says to go ahead and give it a try, to test him. He knew it would be hard for us to grasp. It is a challenge for us to step out and do it, but just like everything else with God, the reward far outweighs the risk.

If your income is low, now is the best time to develop the habit. For some reason, it is a lot easier to begin by tithing ten dollars out of one hundred than it is five hundred out of five thousand. If you start with the ten dollars or one hundred dollars or wherever you are right now, you will have already developed the habit by the time you get to the five thousand. If your income is already high, then you will just have to take the step of faith and trust God with your money more than you trust yourself. You have probably already experienced putting your money into a pocket with holes in it and having it disappear. Part of the blessing God promised us when we tithe is to guard our crops and protect us from the devourer.

> And I will rebuke the devourer for your sakes.
>
> Malachi 3:11 (NKJV)

If you are tired of watching your money disappear by repairing and replacing your belongings continually, learn to be a tither. God has promised you his blessing and protection.

2. *Pay Your Bills*–This might seem like a funny place to bring that up. You're probably wondering, *What does paying my bills have to do with making God my number-one priority?* Just this: God expects us to be people of honesty, integrity, and obedience. If we have areas in our life that are deceitful and fraudulent, then it doesn't represent God very well and gets in the way of our relationship with him. So after our tithes are paid, we need to pay our bills, make our mortgage or rent payments; pay for our utilities; make our car payments; pay our credit-card payments; pay for our cell phones, cable TV, the Internet, and whatever else we've committed ourselves to.

> Woe to him who builds his house by unrighteousness and his chambers by injustice, who uses his neighbor's service without wages and gives him nothing for his work.
>
> Jeremiah 22:13 (NKJV)

> For listen! Hear the cries of the field workers whom you have cheated of their pay. The wages you held back cry out against you. The cries of those who harvest your fields have reached the ears of the Lord of Heaven's Armies.
>
> James 5:4 (NLT)

If you've made the agreement to receive the goods or the services from somebody, then you are obligated to pay for it. If you don't, that is fraud. If you have allowed yourself to get buried in a deep hole of debt, then make the commitment right now to dig yourself out. You may need to seek help from a Christian financial advisor. Many churches have them on staff. Ask your pastor; he'll be able to connect you with the right person. With God's help and some earnest discipline, you will overcome that debt.

My dad was a very good man and a good father, but in this area of his finances, he had his priorities exactly backwards. After he cashed his paycheck, he would go straight to the grocery store to make sure his family was taken care of. Then if he had enough left over, he would pay the bills. If on the rare occasion there was anything left after that, he would put a few dollars in the offering plate. To his thinking he was doing the best he could with his limited funds to make sure his family was taken care of and his bills were paid. This is how most of the world thinks, and it seems like the most logical way to do things. However, the result of his financial priority list was a lifetime of struggle and barely getting by.

God does not do things according to the logic of this world. Remember he lives in the spiritual world and he operates by spiritual principles. He wants us to learn to operate by spiritual principles as well. He wants us to set aside our logical, analytical, rational, worldly way of figuring things out and live by faith and obedience to his ways.

Here is how my dad should have done things. First he should have taken his pay and separated out his tithes. That is the first fruit, and it belongs to God. If we spend it, we are stealing from God.

> Honor the LORD with your possessions, and with the firstfruits of all your increase; so your barns will be filled with plenty, and your vats will overflow with new wine.
>
> Proverbs 3:9 (NKJV)

Most of us have our paychecks deposited directly in the bank now, so the first thing we need to do is write out our tithe check and subtract it from our account before we pay anything else. Just a quick note here: your tithe is on your gross pay. That is how much you earned before Uncle Sam and everybody else got their hands on your money.

After the tithes were paid, my dad should have paid his bills. Remember, he had the obligation to pay them because he had made the agreements. This is where it gets hard and where we are learning to be obedient to God's Word and live by faith. When you follow this order with your finances, God will be faithful to his Word. Whatever is left after you pay your tithe and pay your bills, God will bless. If it is one hundred dollars, if it is twenty dollars or if it is only five dollars, God is going to take care of you. If you commit to that lifestyle, God is going to bless your finances in ways you can't even imagine.

> But seek first the kingdom of God and His righteousness, and all these things shall be added to you.
>
> Matthew 6:33 (NKJV)

This is where your family obligations fit in also: things like new shoes, haircuts, and school clothes and home and car repairs. You name it. We all know the list is endless, but the point is to make sure you take care of your family the very best you can.

3. *Give Offerings*–It is important that we learn to live a life of giving. This could come in various forms. It could be ministries you feel an attachment to, either from inside your church or outside. It could be charities like medical research or taking care of the poor or disabled, or disaster relief. It could be helping individuals you come in contact with who are in need. There are many opportunities to be a giver; the only constraint is to be wise. Just as we were talking about earlier, check it out, use common sense. There are plenty of con men out there willing to take your money if you are willing to give it to them. Pray about your giving. God will let you know whom to give to

and how much to give. And he will bless your faithfulness and good heart.

> But this I say: He who sows sparingly will also reap sparingly, and he who sows bountifully will also reap bountifully. So let each one give as he purposes in his heart, not grudgingly or of necessity; for God loves a cheerful giver. And God is able to make all grace abound toward you, that you, always having all sufficiency in all things, may have an abundance for every good work.
>
> 2 Corinthians 9:6–8 (NKJV)

4. *Savings and Investment*–Just one more comment about our money I want to mention. This is an important element of our finances that many of us neglect. I'm not a finance or investment expert, so I am not going to tell you how to save or what to invest in; but it is important to do your homework, seek help from experts, then find ways to invest and save. In my experience the easiest way to accomplish this is to have funds taken directly out of your paycheck before you get your hands on them. If you wait until everything else is paid to set some aside, you will never do it. We still have to be wise and remember we still have to pay our tithes and pay our bills, but make the decision now to invest and save for your future.

2. The next item on your priority list is your marriage.

Marriage is God's idea, and it is very important to him. He lays out some pretty specific instructions in his Word for having a good marriage. His plan is for us to do well in our marriages so we are there as a support for each other in surviving this ordeal we call life. However, he wants us to do more than survive; he wants us to thrive. He set up a plan where a man and a woman can come together, learn to live as one, and, as a single unit, conquer the world together.

It is a challenge, though; it is not easy bringing two distinct and separate people together, with different genders, personalities, and backgrounds. We each have our own uniqueness that now needs to be blended together so we can become something better together than we were alone. God wants us to put a priority on it. He wants us to take the time and make the effort to make our marriages work.

For women this comes a little bit easier than it does for men. Not the making-it-work part, the willingness to work at it. Women are naturally relationship-oriented and have the drive to make their relationships better, at least for a while. A woman can get tired of trying if she feels as though she is alone in the effort and will eventually give up the struggle.

Men on the other hand, are normally not very good at relationships. They are achievement- and goal-oriented and most of the time do not see the point of working at their marriage. Relationships do not come naturally for them, and they do not usually like to be put in the position where they have to spend time thinking about them. Most of the time, men are not going to be really excited to read a book about marriage, attend a marriage class, or go to a marriage retreat.

Since they are achievement-driven, and they gain

self-esteem from the things they accomplish, they also do not like to be made to feel incompetent. That is what they think about going to marriage counseling or classes; they know they are not good at it, so they are going to feel inadequate and messed up. It's not so much that they don't want to feel that way; it's that they don't want to feel that way in front of others. They don't want to get put on the spot and be embarrassed.

Ladies, you can have a huge impact on your husbands if you do it right. They will not respond to nagging, criticizing, or complaining. You need to treat your husband the way God told you to.

> And let the wife see that she respects her husband.
>
> Ephesians 5:33 (NKJV)

Your husband wants more than anything for you to think he is *all that.* However, if you want him to be *all that,* you are going to have to build it into him. He is not going to get there on his own. The first thing you can do is follow God's example of how he accomplishes things.

> God, who gives life to the dead and calls those things which do not exist as though they did.
>
> Romans 4:17 (NKJV)

You'd be surprised how easy your husband is to mold and shape. Start by saying good things to him and about him. Tell him what a good man he is and how much you admire him. Tell him what a good husband and what a good father he is. In some instances you might be stretching the truth a little, but remember you're speaking things into existence just as God does. Deep down inside he does want to be those things, and as you speak them, he will try to live up to them. You might not see the change overnight, but if you give him time, he'll get there. And acknowledge it when he does do something right. He'll like the feeling and try to get it again. One more thing: become your husband's PR rep. Don't tell anyone, especially your relatives and friends, how messed up your husband is. Only tell them the good things. Make them believe your husband is the greatest man on earth. It reflects better on you anyway. Why do you want the whole world to think you were so dumb you got married to an idiot?

Men, God wants you to make your marriage a priority. I know it doesn't come naturally for you, and you don't see what the big deal is; but it's important to God, so it should be important to you. Here is what the Bible says:

> Husbands, love your wives, just as Christ also loved the church and gave Himself for her.
>
> Ephesians 5:25 (NKJV)

> So husbands ought to love their own wives as their own bodies; he who loves his wife loves himself.
>
> Ephesians 5:28 (NKJV)

> Nevertheless let each one of you in particular so love his own wife as himself.
>
> Ephesians 5:33 (NKJV)

Do you think Paul is trying to tell us something? He says it three times in the same chapter: "Husbands, love your wives." You would think we would get it!

Okay, what does that mean to love our wives? God had to spell that out for us in the form of a command because he knew we wouldn't do it unless he told us to. As I said it's just not the natural way we think about things. Have you ever wondered why our wives normally don't really develop a bunch of outside interests as we do? We like softball, cars, hunting, fishing, golf, football; we've got so much stuff we like to do. We're just so well rounded.

But what do our wives do? They do have an interest like that, you know; it's their husbands and their families. Their hobby is us! And they want us to feel the same way about them. They want to be the most important part of our life. It's not that they don't want us to do things; they just want to feel they are more important to us than all that stuff we're involved in. I know it sounds hard, but if we make the effort to make our wives feel loved, they will want us to do some of the stuff we like to do; maybe not all of it, but at least some of it. Your relationship with God is the only thing in this world more important than your wife. Men, do yourself a favor, love your wife!

Here's some things we can do to let our wives know how important they are to us: We can take the time to read some books about marriage and relationships. We know we're not good at it. Why not take some positive steps to get better? While we're at it, we can take her to some marriage classes or attend a marriage conference or retreat with her. And if you have some real tough issues you need to deal with, be willing to go to counseling with her. If we make the effort and are willing to try, it is amazing what God can do with our marriages.

3. Next are your children.

Notice they are not ahead of our marriages. Many people make the mistake of putting their children at the top of their priority list but that is out of order. Our kids are very important, but the best way to make sure they are treated well and taken care of is to make sure our relationship with God is right and to make sure our marriages are working. If we do those things right, everything else will fall into place.

There are some things that children need from their parents, though. For children their parents are everything. Their parents are their total source, their total security, and their total sense of well-being. As they get older, children's demands in each of these areas will lessen to some extent, but, as parents, we need to keep in mind when we decided to have children, we signed on for the long haul.

The first thing I mentioned was their source. Our children come into this world with nothing, and they have no way of acquiring or generating anything without us. We are responsible for everything they have: their food, clothes, shelter, furniture, and toys. Because they are totally helpless and completely vulnerable, they move straight to the top of our priority list. This is where we have to be careful because we will be tempted to not pay our tithes and let our bills go because of things the children need or the other household expenses that continually pop up. Where the kids' needs go on our lists is ahead of ourselves, not God. God requires that we take care of and support our families and make sure all of their needs are met.

> But if anyone does not provide for his own, and especially for those of his household, he has denied the faith and is worse than an unbeliever.
>
> 1 Timothy 5:8 (NKJV)

The next thing is a child's security. Children need to feel safe and protected in their homes and in their families. That means safe from physical harm, safe from emotional harm, and safe from spiritual harm. There are many threats to our children in this world. As a parent, we need to be on guard continually. We need to monitor their television time, their computer time, their friends and their friends' families, the places our children go, and the things they do. They don't have the knowledge or the experience to recognize the threats to their safety; we do. That's why we need to be vigilant in our protection of them.

Some parents make the mistake of letting their guard down a little when their children reach their teenage years. That can be a costly decision.

Our kids think they are so smart and that they have life all figured out, but they don't. As they get older and start to make a few choices on their own, their lack of experience can take them places and get them involved with things they should never be involved with. If anything, you should step up your vigilance when they get to junior high and then high school. Oh sure, they will get mad, throw a fit, and probably call you names, but remember: you're the parent. The responsibility of raising those kids was given to you by God, and he is going to hold you accountable for how it all turns out.

Most parents understand the importance of protecting their children from threats outside the home, but unfortunately many of our children have to suffer from pain that comes from inside their homes. You were given to your children by God to nurture, protect, and guide them to the fulfilling and successful life he designed for them. If the biggest threat to your child's safety and security comes from you, then you need to get help quick. You are causing damage to their emotional well-being that they might never recover from.

Children's sense of well-being comes from their families and their home life. There has been a deceptive and fraudulent philosophy imposed on our society over the last few years. It is the concept of quality time versus quantity time. Because of our busy lives, split homes, and selfish lifestyles, we have come up with the thought that if we can't spend a lot of time with our children we can at least make our short time together really count for something. It sounds real good, but the problem is, to our children, there is no such thing as quality time. They just need to spend time with us. A lot of time with us. We, as parents, need to set aside all of the things we want to be involved with and go home. We do have to work for a living and provide for our families. But when work is over and the shopping is done, we need to go home and spend time with our families. Have you ever come home, had your kids run up and greet you at the door, get a kiss and hug, and then run off down the street to play? That is actually all they need most of the time, just to know we're around; they get security from that. We do need to spend time reading with them, playing games, or just wrestling in the backyard, but most of the time all they need is to know we're at home.

Another big part of our children's well-being is our marriages. Divorce is one of the biggest worries in a child's life. Instead of arguing and fighting, they need to see us kissing and hugging. When we set an example for our kids of how good a marriage should be, they'll carry that into their own marriages when they grow up.

One more thing our children need from us is consistency. The biggest thing children rebel against is hypocrisy in their parents and other adults in their lives. We cannot tell them to act one way while we are acting another. They need consistency between what we say and how we act. They also need consistency in the messages and lessons they receive from other adults in their lives. That is why being in church is so important. If the lessons they receive from their Sunday school teachers, children's church leaders, and youth pastors is the same message they are getting at home from you, then the principles of living right and making good choices will get imbedded deep within their hearts. Good attitudes, proper values, and high standards will be with them throughout their lifetimes.

> Train up a child in the way he should go, and when he is old he will not depart from it.
>
> Proverbs 22:6 (NKJV)

4. Now comes your job.

For those of you who are workaholics, notice that your relationship with God, church, your marriage, and your children all come before your job. For some of us, that is a real challenge. In our minds the reason we are working is to take care of our families, and they need to understand that all this work we are doing is for them.

Others of us have a hard time finding and then keeping a job. We think you've got to know somebody or at least be in the right place at the right time to get a good job. When we do finally find a job, we find out the bosses are idiots and our fellow employees are hard to get along with. Only the brownnosers get ahead, you know; that's why they all hate me and why I got fired. I wasn't willing to kiss up.

Balance is the key. Satan loves extremes. God loves balance. Satan wants to get us off track and messed up on one side or the other. We need to find balance though. God wants us to work. He wants us to earn a living and support ourselves and our families. Did you know God gave Adam a job before he gave him a wife? He had to meet, study, and name all of animals

God had created. After he finished all that, God gave him a wife. Young ladies should keep that in mind when they are agreeing to become some young man's wife. You need to let him know that he better be able to get a job and keep it if he wants you to be part of his life.

God also says if we want to eat we need to have a job.

> For even when we were with you, we commanded you this: If anyone will not work, neither shall he eat.
>
> 2 Thessalonians 3:10 (NKJV)

If you need training, get the training. If you need education, get the education. Do what it takes to put yourself in a position to take care of your family. We already looked at this verse once, but it is worth repeating. God wants you to take care of your family.

> But if anyone does not provide for his own, and especially for those of his household, he has denied the faith and is worse than an unbeliever.
>
> 1 Timothy 5:8 (NKJV)

On the other side of the coin are those who work too much. This is where balance comes in. God wants you to drop your work down your priority list just a little. Hard work is good, and it is important, just not so important it takes away from your relationship with God and time with your family. It is okay if there are seasons of hard work, when your long hours are only for a specific period of time. Then when they come to an end, you will be able to spend time with and reconnect to your family. However, if those long hours go on for months or even years and your kids are growing up without even knowing who you are, then it might be time to consider a career change. I know that sounds good and easy for me to say from here, but ask God for direction; he'll show you what to do. Be willing to follow his lead and direction when he shows you.

5. Then comes your ministry.

You might be thinking, *I don't have a ministry. What is he talking about?* Well, we need to be involved in ministry. This is what I was talking about earlier when I said we need to be active in our churches. When we are new to Christianity, we have a while to learn and grow before we need to get involved. But once we have been in church for a little while, we need to start looking for ways to get busy. Running and maintaining a church, managing the services, and operating the church ministries are big jobs, and there is always room for people willing to help. We need to be willing to go to work wherever we are needed, then work hard and be faithful at whatever we are asked to do.

I mentioned in the introduction to this book that my wife and I have worked in just about every department in our church over the years. All of that is how we got to where we are now. In each one of the jobs, we learned, we grew, and all that time we were changing. We learned what we liked, what we didn't like, what we were good at, and some things we were not so good at. Through all of that, God was molding us and shaping us and turning us into the people he wants us to be. He was helping us understand our design, our purpose, and what he wants to do with our lives. And he's not through with us yet; we still have a lot of molding and shaping and discovering to go through.

That is how it will be for you. As you get involved in ministry, God will take you through the same process we went through. You will learn and grow and change. It will be amazing to you and everyone around what God does with you. The only thing you have to do to get there is don't quit. You will make mistakes; the people you work around and for will make mistakes, but don't let any of that stop you or hold you back. Just keep on plugging away. God is going to do great things in your life.

One mistake Christians make is confusing their work for God with their relationship with God. Our relationship with God is at the top of our priority list. It is where we spend time with God and develop that intimate relationship we were designed for. We do the work for God when our other priorities are taken care of. We have to take the time to make our marriages work, we need to make sure we are meeting the needs of our children, and we need to be successful at our jobs. When all those are taken care of, we can find a ministry or job at church to be involved with. It is common for people, especially new Christians, to get involved in too many areas of ministry and neglect the other areas of their lives.

There are a few Christians, actually a very small minority, that have their job also be their ministry.

These people need to be especially careful. It is too easy and unfortunately all too common for those in full-time ministry to neglect their marriages and their families at the expense of their work for God. We need to remember that our marriages, our family life, and the well-being of our children are our number-one ministry. It is the area of our lives that God will hold us accountable for before any of the work we do for him.

6. Last on our priority list is pleasure and entertainment.

So many in today's culture put this right at the top of their list. It's not that God doesn't want us to have any fun or recreation; he just wants us to make sure we are living up to our responsibilities first. I love to have fun, and I love to be entertained. I just need to make sure my money and my time is dedicated to my marriage, my family, and my obligations before it is spent on golf, baseball, the movies, or whatever else I want to do for fun.

When our tithes are paid, our bills are paid, and our family's needs are met, we can go have all the fun we want. We can go on cruises, go to Disneyland, or go to the South Pacific if our obligations are met first. If you don't have quite enough income after your responsibilities are taken care of to do those kinds of things yet, then you will have to find cheaper forms of entertainment. There's plenty of fun stuff to do out there that doesn't cost much money. But if you spend the time and the money to play on a softball team, or play golf, or go shopping for new clothes or new shoes but your marriage, your family, your job, or your relationship with God is being neglected, your life is out of order. As long as you live like that, you will continue to struggle, and if you continue and never do change, you will stand in front of God one day and answer for your wrong choices.

Learn to be Excellent

Now that you have your priority list in order, learn to be *excellent* at everything you do. Being excellent means doing your very best. There are many stories in the Bible of men and women who stood out from the crowd because of their honesty, their integrity, and their faith in God. Noah, Abraham, Joseph, Moses, Joshua, Ruth, Esther, Job, Nehemiah, David, Elijah, Jeremiah, and Daniel, just to name a few. The list goes on and on. These people didn't get recognized because they were the biggest, the strongest, or the smartest. They excelled because they did their best at whatever situation they found themselves in and because they listened to the voice of God and followed the leading of the Holy Spirit. Here is what the Bible says about Daniel:

> Inasmuch as an excellent spirit, knowledge, understanding ... were found in this Daniel.
>
> Daniel 5:12 (NKJV)

That is how God wants us to be. He wants us to have an excellent spirit. That means we do our best at whatever we find ourselves doing.

> Whatever your hand finds to do, do it with your might.
>
> Ecclesiastes 9:10 (NKJV)

> And whatever you do, do it heartily, as to the Lord and not to men.
>
> Colossians 3:23 (NKJV)

We have a tendency to be sloppy and lazy, but God wants us to work hard and be excellent. We need to learn to be excellent at whatever we do. Part of being excellent is taking care of what we have. We don't necessarily need to have the biggest and most beautiful house or the fanciest and most expensive car, but we need to take care of what we have. We need to clean our houses and have things picked up and put away. We need to keep our cars clean both inside and out.

Christians should be the best—the best at work, the best at school, the best at church, and the best at home. There should be something different about us that stands out from those around us.

Conclusion

I hope I've given you some new things to think about and some new ways of looking at things. As I have mentioned before, we are all works in progress and are at different stages of development. Hopefully we are all growing, committed to change, and learning to listen to the leading of the Holy Spirit in our lives each day.

God has a plan and a destiny designed especially for you. The only thing that will keep you from reaching it is if you quit.

> And let us not grow weary while doing good, for in due season we shall reap if we do not lose heart.
> Galatians 6:9 (NKJV)

We can't stop living right and making good choices. That verse is telling us that in due season we will reap the harvest of our good choices. The problem is that there is no way of telling when due season will arrive. Only God knows, and he won't tell us. I have known so many new Christians who have come in, turned their lives over to Jesus, and begun the process of changing. But because their life was in such a mess before they came to know Jesus, it is a long process of digging themselves out of that giant hole they find themselves in. I've seen many hang in there and, as the Holy Spirit leads, make the required changes and eventually get back to level ground, then move on to accomplish great things in kingdom of God. I've seen others, though, that never make it. It is such a long, hard road climbing out of the giant pit that they do just what that verse says; they grow weary in doing good. Consequently, due season never arrives, and they never reap their harvest. That is why I say, "Don't quit!" It is the only way you won't make it. Remember it took you a long time to dig that big hole, so it will probably take you a while to get out.

Never forget that you were specifically designed by God with a plan and purpose that only you can fulfill. Don't let the discouragement and circumstances of life hold you back. The Bible calls those who are able to excel at this life and fulfill their destiny "overcomers." You can be one of those because Jesus has made it possible.

In the first three chapters of the book of Revelation, Jesus makes seven promises to those of us who are overcomers. Look those verses up and read them to see if you can find what the promises are. Then in chapter twelve he tells us how it is possible to be an overcomer.

> And they overcame him by the blood of the Lamb and by the word of their testimony.
>
> Revelation 12:11 (NKJV)

We do it through the shed blood of Jesus that defeated sin in our lives and restored our relationship to God. And we do it by the word of our testimony, which is sharing with others the amazing things that Jesus has done in our lives.

Postscript

I once heard a preacher make the statement "I want this message to be more than informational. I want it to be transformational." That is what I want from this book. I have shared a lot of information with you. I hope it has been interesting and informative and that you have learned a lot. But most of all, I hope I have been able to explain Christianity to you in ways that are life changing. I want you to go past just collecting information to turning your information into knowledge, turning your knowledge into understanding, and then turning your understanding into wisdom. Wisdom is acting on the understanding you have gained.

Believe it or not, I have barely scratched the surface of the knowledge available to us in the areas of theology, church doctrine, and Christian living. I mentioned in the introduction that I am not a pastor and not a theologian. Pastors and theologians will look at my book and realize that there is so much this book doesn't cover. The pastors will be thinking of all the sermons that need to be preached and the theologian about all the books that need to be written to cover all this material thoroughly. This book is written to give you just a basic understanding. I am challenging you to become a student of learning the ways of God and then a master of applying all of that learning to your life. Read all the books of the pastors and the theologians you can find, listen to their sermons, get all of their CDs and DVDs , and make sure you are in church every time the doors are open. Hosea 4:6 says, "My people are destroyed for lack of knowledge" (NKJV). Determine in your heart that this is not going to be you. We live in the information age, so the knowledge and information is out there. Go after it, study it, learn it, change, and grow.

> Study this Book of Instruction continually. Meditate on it day and night so you will be sure to obey everything written in it. Only then will you prosper and succeed in all you do.
>
> Joshua 1:8 (NLT)

I can't stress to you enough how important being in church is. It is where your strength and encouragement will come from. It will be very difficult for you to survive in your Christian walk without the support of your fellow believers. You can't wake up every Sunday morning and decide whether or not you are going to church that day. If you do that, your attendance will be very sporadic at best and eventually fade away all together. Make the decision right now for you and your family and commit to it.

> But as for me and my house, we will serve the LORD.
>
> Joshua 24:15 (NKJV)

Be just like Joshua and say, "From this day forward, we are going to be in church." Just think of all the stress that will eliminate in your life by making that decision once instead of fifty-two times a year. If you want to flourish in your life, get yourself and your family planted in the house of God.

> Those who are planted in the house of the LORD shall flourish in the courts of our God. They shall still bear fruit in old age; they shall be fresh and flourishing.
>
> Psalm 92:13–14 (NKJV)

You can't take a plant and continually transplant it and expect it to survive for very long. So many Christians just seem to hop around from church to church and then wonder why they don't see much progress in their Christian growth. One of the mistakes they make is looking too much at people. People will let you down. I've got some bad news for you. Your pastor isn't perfect, the leaders in your church aren't perfect, and, as a matter of fact, none of the people in your church are perfect. They will all say things they shouldn't say, do things they shouldn't do, and they will all let you down if you put too much of your hope and faith in them. We all need to have good leaders and mentors to help us through life. We just can't put such high expectations on them that they can't make a mistake, or we are going to get mad and leave. No one can live up to that.

When Jesus lived on earth, he spent three years with his disciples before he left them in the care of the Holy Spirit and went back to heaven. That is a good time frame for you to live by too. If you are new to Christianity and this whole God and church thing, commit to at least three years in the church where you made your decision to give your life to Christ. There are probably some exceptions to that, but if you have found a church with good people and a pastor that preaches the Word, stay there until a firm foundation has been established for your life. After the three years have passed, you will be in a better position to make a decision on your church home.

Let me repeat what I said earlier: "Don't quit!" The only thing that will cause you to fail is quitting. You hang in there with God, and God will hang in there with you.

To learn more from Alan Kelly, visit Forever Together Marriage Ministries at www.forevertogetheronline.com.

Bibliography

Pearlman, Myer. *Knowing the Doctrines of the Bible.* Gospel Publishing House, Springfield, MO. 1937.

Spirit-Filled Life Bible, General Editor, Jack W Hayford, Litt.D. Copyright © 1999 by Thomas Nelson, Inc. New King James Version®. Copyright © 1982 by Thomas Nelson, Inc.

The Thompson Chain-Reference Bible, Compiled and Edited by Frank Charles Thompson, D.D., PH.D. B.B. Kirkbride Bible Co., Inc. Indianapolis, Ind. Copyright © 1964. King James Version.

Stern, David H. *Complete Jewish Bible.* Jewish New Testament Publications, Clarksville, MD. 1998.

www.newadvent.org. *Catholic Encyclopedia.*

www.en.wikipedia.org. *Henry VIII, Mary I, Elizabeth I, James I.*

www.williamtyndale.com. *The Tyndale Gallery.*

Foxe, John. *Foxe's Book of Martyrs.* Edited by William Byron Forbush. Electronic Edition STEP Files Copyright © 1999, The Learning Company, Inc. Originally published in 1563 by John Day.

Arno, Richard Gene, Ph.D. Arno, Phyllis Jean, Ph.D. *Creation Therapy: A Biblically Based Model for Christian Counseling,* Fifth Edition. Arno, Sarasota, FL. Copyright © 1993.

Littauer, Florence. *Personality Plus: How to Understand Others by Understanding Yourself.* Fleming H. Revell, Baker Book House, Grand Rapids, MI. 1992.

Mossholder, Ray. *Marriage Plus: The Bible and Marriage.* Creation House, Lake Mary, FL. 1990.

Smalley, Gary. *If He Only Knew: A Valuable Guide to Knowing, Understanding, and Loving Your Wife.* Zondervan Publishing House, Grand Rapids, MI. 1988.

Smalley, Gary. *For Better or Best: Understanding Your Man.* Zondervan Publishing House, Grand Rapids, MI. 1988.

Snyder, Chuck. *Men: Some Assembly Required, a Woman's Guide to Understanding Her Man.* Tyndale House Publishers, Wheaton, IL. 1995.

Snyder, Chuck. *The Way to a Woman's Heart: A Road Map to a Successful Marriage.* Multnomah Publishers, Sisters, OR. 2000.

Farrel, Bill and Pam, *Men Are Like Waffles—Woman Are Like Spaghetti: Understanding and Delighting in Your Differences.* Harvest House Publishers, Eugene, OR. 2001.

www.articles.health.msn.com. *The New Sex Scorecard,* Psychology Today.com. 2005.

Treat, Casey D. *Renewing the Mind: The Foundation of Your Success,* Harrison House, Inc. Tulsa, OK. 1999.

Hagin, Kenneth E. *The Believer's Authority.* Faith Library Publications, Tulsa, OK. 1985.

Hagin, Kenneth E. *Plans, Purposes, and Pursuits.* Faith Library Publications, Tulsa, OK. 1988.

End Notes

1. www.williamtyndale.com. *The Tyndale Gallery.*
2. Foxe, John. *Foxe's Book of Martyrs.* Edited by William Byron Forbush. Electronic Edition STEP Files Copyright © 1999, The Learning Company, Inc. Originally published in 1563 by John Day.
3. The Newsboys, *Going Public,* "Real Good Thing," lyrics by Steve Taylor & Peter Furler, music by Jody Davis & Peter Furler © 1994 Ariose Music (a division of Star Song Communications, admin. by Gaither Copyright Management), Warner Alliance Music, Soylent Tunes & Helmet Publishing.
4. Arno, Richard Gene, Ph.D. Arno, Phyllis Jean, Ph.D. *Creation Therapy: A Biblically Based Model for Christian Counseling,* Fifth Edition. Arno, Sarasota, FL. Copyright © 1993.
5. Farrel, Bill and Pam, *Men Are Like Waffles—Woman Are Like Spaghetti: Understanding and Delighting in Your Differences.* Harvest House Publishers, Eugene, OR. 2001.
6. www.wisdomquotes.com, Copyright © 1995–2009 Jone Johnson Lewis. All Rights Reserved.